STEP 3

Let's Practice More!

문법 내용을 제대로 이해했는지 확인할 수 있도록 SET 01~08까지 다양한 유형의 연습문제를 실었어요. 문제를 하나하나 풀다보면 해당 UNIT의 핵심 개념을 제대로 익히게 될 거예요.

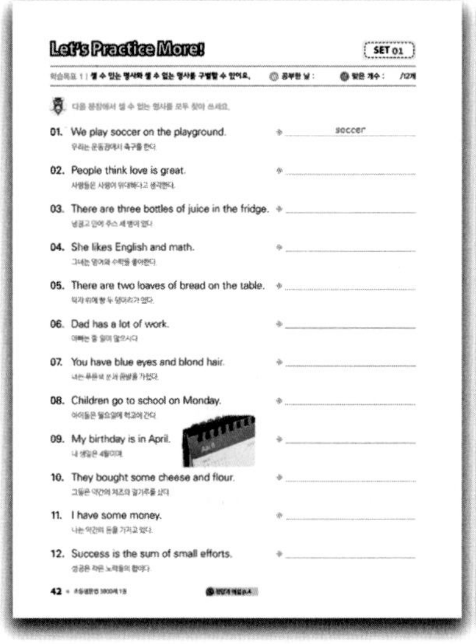
Let's Practice More! SET 01

01. We play soccer on the playground. → soccer
02. People think love is great.
03. There are three bottles of juice in the fridge.
04. She likes English and math.
05. There are two loaves of bread on the table.
06. Dad has a lot of work.
07. You have blue eyes and blond hair.
08. Children go to school on Monday.
09. My birthday is in April.
10. They bought some cheese and flour.
11. I have some money.
12. Success is the sum of small efforts.

42

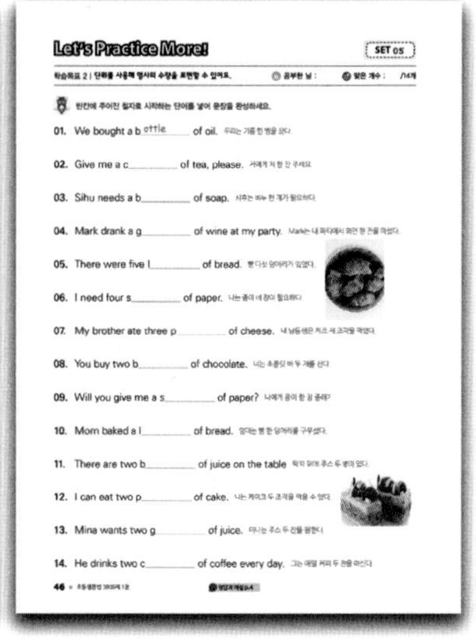
Let's Practice More! SET 05

01. We bought a bottle of oil.
02. Give me a c_______ of tea, please.
03. Sihu needs a b_______ of soap.
04. Mark drank a g_______ of wine at my party.
05. There were five l_______ of bread.
06. I need four s_______ of paper.
07. My brother ate three p_______ of cheese.
08. You buy two b_______ of chocolate.
09. Will you give me a s_______ of paper?
10. Mom baked a l_______ of bread.
11. There are two b_______ of juice on the table.
12. I can eat two p_______ of cake.
13. Mina wants two g_______ of juice.
14. He drinks two c_______ of coffee every day.

46

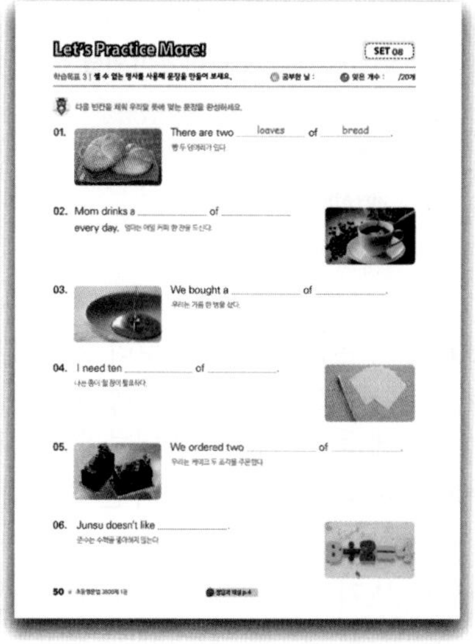
Let's Practice More! SET 08

01. There are two loaves of bread.
02. Mom drinks a _______ of _______ every day.
03. We bought a _______ of _______.
04. I need ten _______ of _______.
05. We ordered two _______ of _______.
06. Junsu doesn't like _______.

50

STEP 4

마무리 실전테스트

최종 마무리 테스트로서 권당 2회분의 실전테스트를 실었어요. 총 30문제의 진단평가 및 교내평가 유형의 실전문제로 앞에서 배운 내용을 복습하고 취약한 부분을 파악해 봐요.

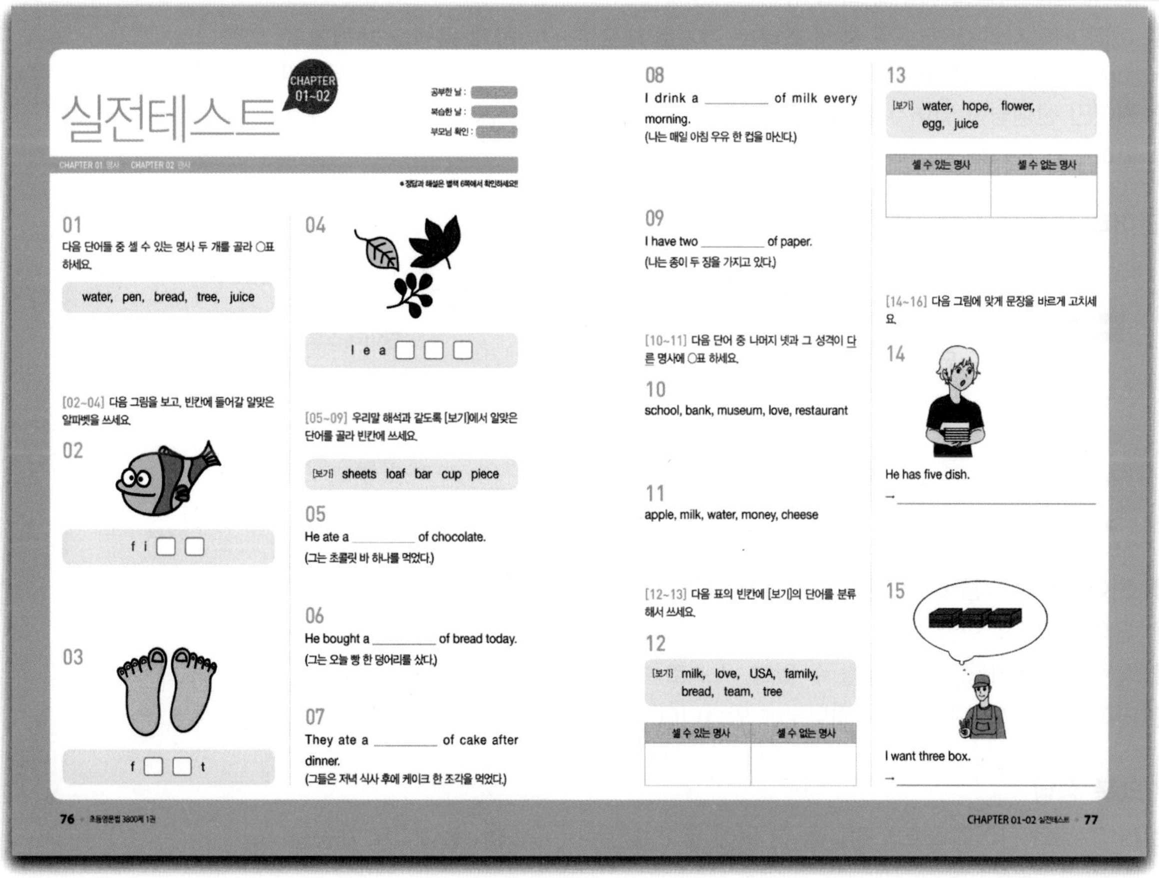
실전테스트 CHAPTER 01~02

공부한 날 :
복습한 날 :
부모님 확인 :

CHAPTER 01 명사 CHAPTER 02 명사

* 정답과 해설은 별책 6쪽에서 확인하세요!

01
다음 단어들 중 셀 수 있는 명사 두 개를 골라 ○표 하세요.

water, pen, bread, tree, juice

[02~04] 다음 그림을 보고, 빈칸에 들어갈 알맞은 알파벳을 쓰세요.

02
f i □ □

03
f □ □ t

04
l e a □ □ □

[05~09] 우리말 해석과 같도록 [보기]에서 알맞은 단어를 골라 빈칸에 쓰세요.

[보기] sheets loaf bar cup piece

05
He ate a _______ of chocolate.
(그는 초콜릿 바 하나를 먹었다.)

06
He bought a _______ of bread today.
(그는 오늘 빵 한 덩어리를 샀다.)

07
They ate a _______ of cake after dinner.
(그들은 저녁 식사 후에 케이크 한 조각을 먹었다.)

08
I drink a _______ of milk every morning.
(나는 매일 아침 우유 한 컵을 마신다.)

09
I have two _______ of paper.
(나는 종이 두 장을 가지고 있다.)

[10~11] 다음 단어 중 나머지 넷과 그 성격이 다른 명사에 ○표 하세요.

10
school, bank, museum, love, restaurant

11
apple, milk, water, money, cheese

[12~13] 다음 표의 빈칸에 [보기]의 단어를 분류해서 쓰세요.

12
[보기] milk, love, USA, family, bread, team, tree

셀 수 있는 명사	셀 수 없는 명사

13
[보기] water, hope, flower, egg, juice

셀 수 있는 명사	셀 수 없는 명사

[14~16] 다음 그림에 맞게 문장을 바르게 고치세요.

14
He has five dish.
→ _______

15
I want three box.
→ _______

76 초등영문법 3800제 1권

CHAPTER 01-02 실전테스트 77

워크북 구성 및 활용법 워크북은 아래와 같은 방법으로 활용하세요.

1. 단어쓰기 연습

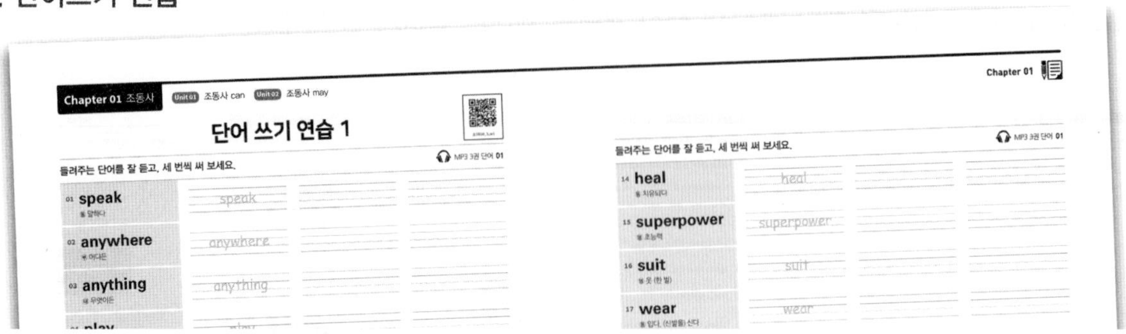

❶ 먼저 본문 학습을 마무리 합니다.
❷ 해당 페이지의 QR코드를 통해 스마트 기기로 빠르고 편리하게 음원을 재생할 수 있습니다. 전체 음원 파일은 마더텅 홈페이지(www.toptutor.co.kr)에서 다운로드 가능합니다.
❸ 원어민 선생님이 읽어주는 영단어를 잘 듣고 안내선 안에 영어 단어 철자를 세 번씩 쓰세요.

2. 받아쓰기 시험 (Dictation Test)

❶ 먼저 본문 학습을 마무리 합니다.
❷ 해당 페이지의 QR코드를 통해 스마트 기기로 빠르고 편리하게 음원을 재생할 수 있습니다. 전체 음원 파일은 마더텅 홈페이지(www.toptutor.co.kr)에서 다운로드 가능합니다.
❸ 원어민 선생님이 읽어주는 문장을 잘 듣고, 빈칸을 채우세요.
❹ 받아쓰기 정답은 워크북 뒷부분에 있습니다.

3. 단어테스트

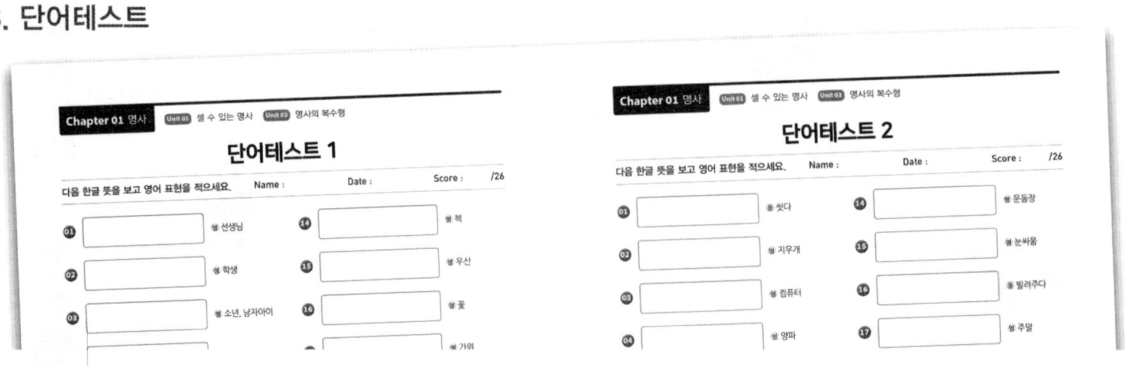

❶ 단어쓰기 연습을 하며, 단어들을 암기합니다.
❷ 단어테스트의 한글 뜻을 보고 암기한 영단어를 써 보세요.
❸ 학원에서 평가용으로 활용할 수 있고, 스스로 확인하는 용도로 활용할 수도 있습니다.
❹ 단어테스트 정답은 워크북 뒷부분에 있습니다.

4. 워크북 정답

Dictation Test와 단어테스트의 정답을 한 눈에 알아보기 쉬운 형태의 정답지로 제공합니다.

영문법 판매 1위, 중학영문법 3800제의 초등시리즈

초등영문법 3800제

LEVEL 3

기초1단계 CONTENTS

본문 목차			페이지
Chapter 01 조동사	Unit 01	조동사 can	p.8
	Unit 02	조동사 may	p.10
	Unit 03	조동사 must, have to (1)	p.30
	Unit 04	조동사 must, have to (2)	p.32
Chapter 02 형용사	Unit 01	형용사의 종류와 역할 (1)	p.54
	Unit 02	형용사의 종류와 역할 (2)	p.56
Chapter 03 부사	Unit 01	부사의 기능과 모양	p.78
	Unit 02	주의해야 할 부사 / 빈도부사	p.80
실전테스트 Chapter 01 - 03			p.100
Chapter 04 감탄문	Unit 01	What으로 시작하는 감탄문	p.106
	Unit 02	How로 시작하는 감탄문	p.108
Chapter 05 명령문	Unit 01	긍정 명령문	p.130
	Unit 02	부정 명령문	p.132
Chapter 06 청유문	Unit 01	청유문	p.154
	Unit 02	제안을 나타내는 다른 표현	p.156
실전테스트 Chapter 04 - 06			p.176

워크북 목차		페이지
워크북	단어쓰기연습	p.182
	Dictation Test	p.210
	단어테스트	p.224
	워크북 정답	p.238

Chapter 01 조동사

이 챕터에서는 be동사나 일반동사의 앞에 붙어서 의미를 더해주는
동사인 '조동사'에 대해 배워 보아요.

☆ 학습 방향 및 배울 내용 미리보기 ☆

☐ **Unit 01 : I can speak English.**

조동사 can

조동사의 특징과 조동사 can의 용법과 부정형에 대해 알아보아요.

▼

☐ **Unit 02 : May I help you?**

조동사 may

조동사 may의 용법과 조동사를 사용하여 허락이나 요청을 하는 방법을 알아보아요.

▼

☐ **Unit 03 : You must[have to] choose.**

조동사 must, have to (1)

조동사 must, have to의 용법과 시제와 주어에 따른 형태 변화를 알아보아요.

▼

☐ **Unit 04 : We must not tell lies.**

조동사 must, have to (2)

조동사 must, have to의 부정형에 대해 알아보아요.

단어 미리보기

이 챕터에 나올 단어들 중 이미 알고 있는 단어가 있나요?
맞는 뜻을 골라 체크해 봐요.

날짜 : 이름 : 알고 있는 단어의 수 : /24개

No.	아는 단어	단어	품사	알맞은 뜻에 체크 표시해 봐요.			
1	☑	something	대명사	어떤 것	☑	특별한 것	☐
2	☐	shoot	동사	밟다	☐	쏘다	☐
3	☐	wear	동사	입다	☐	벗다	☐
4	☐	leave	동사	남다	☐	떠나다	☐
5	☐	answer	명사	질문	☐	대답	☐
6	☐	exam	명사	시험	☐	결과	☐
7	☐	believe	동사	거짓말하다	☐	믿다	☐
8	☐	change	동사	취소하다	☐	바꾸다	☐
9	☐	life	명사	삶	☐	거짓말	☐
10	☐	understand	동사	듣지 못하다	☐	이해하다	☐
11	☐	win	동사	이기다	☐	지다	☐
12	☐	picture	명사	예술	☐	그림	☐
13	☐	wash	동사	벗다	☐	씻다	☐
14	☐	get up	동사	일어나다	☐	깨우다	☐
15	☐	near	전치사	~에서 멀리	☐	~에서 가까이	☐
16	☐	animal	명사	동물	☐	식물	☐
17	☐	warm	형용사	차가운	☐	따뜻한	☐
18	☐	lie	명사	진실	☐	거짓말	☐
19	☐	beach	명사	산	☐	해변	☐
20	☐	wait	동사	떠나다	☐	기다리다	☐
21	☐	follow	동사	따르다	☐	훔치다	☐
22	☐	power	명사	힘	☐	종	☐
23	☐	stop	동사	멈추다	☐	계속 가다	☐
24	☐	question	명사	대답	☐	질문	☐

UNIT 01 I can speak English.

❖ POiNT 1 ❖

조동사 동사 앞에 붙어서 be동사나 일반동사에 의미를 더해 도움(助: 도울 조)을 주는 동사를 말해요. 조동사에는 can(~할 수 있다), may(~일지도 모른다), must(~해야 한다), have to(~해야 한다)와 같은 것들이 있어요.

I 나는	speak 말한다	English. 영어를
I 나는	can speak 말할 수 있다	English. 영어를

❖ POiNT 2 ❖

조동사의 특징

You can go anywhere. 넌 어디든지 갈 수 있어.	**조동사 뒤**에는 항상 **동사원형**이 와요.
I can be anything. 난 무엇이든 될 수 있어.	am, are, is가 조동사 뒤에 오면 **be(원형)**로 써요.
I ~~may can~~ swim. ⇨ I can swim. 난 수영할 수 있어.	조동사 두 개를 **함께 쓰지 않아요.**

❖ POiNT 3 ❖

조동사 can (부정형: cannot/ can't)

~할 수 있다 (능력)	I **can** play the guitar. 나는 기타를 연주**할 수 있어**. Come on! You **can** do it! 어서! 넌 **할 수 있어**! I **can't** fix my computer. 난 내 컴퓨터를 고칠 **수 없어**.
~해도 좋다 (허락)	**Can** I say something? 제가 말을 좀 해**도 될까요**? **Can** I have a glass of Coke? 제가 콜라를 한 잔 마셔**도 될까요**?

Check and Write

다음 빈칸에 들어갈 적절한 단어를 보기에서 골라 써 보세요.

1. 보기 goes go went going

You can [go] to Sihu's house.

너는 시후의 집에 가도 좋아.

2. 보기 do doing did does

I can [ ] it!

나는 그것을 할 수 있어!

3. 보기 is are be am

You can [ ] a pilot.

너는 파일럿이 될 수 있어.

4. 보기 can can't

She [ ] play the piano.

그녀는 피아노를 칠 수 있어.

5. 보기 Can Can't

[ ] I have a seat?

제가 앉아도 될까요?

정답과 해설 p.2

UNIT 02 May I help you?

조동사 may

❖ POiNT 1 ❖

조동사 may

~일지도 모른다 (추측)	She may know his name. 그녀는 그의 이름을 알지도 몰라. This may sting a little. 이거 조금 따가울지도 몰라. It may not be true. 그것은 사실이 아닐지도 몰라.	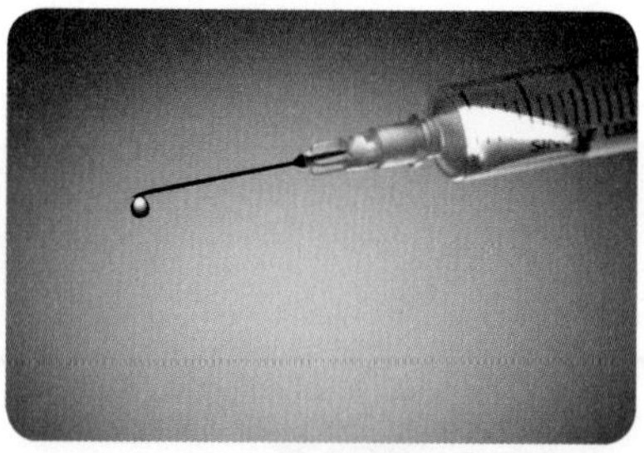
~해도 좋다 (허락)	You may bring your friend. 넌 너의 친구를 데려와도 좋아. May I help you? 제가 당신을 도와드릴까요? May I come in? 제가 들어가도 될까요?	

❖ POiNT 2 ❖

허락이나 요청에 대한 대답

허락/요청의 질문	May[Can] I take a break? 저 쉬어도 될까요?
긍정의 대답	Yes, you may[can]. 그래, 그러렴. Sure. / Of course. 물론이지.
부정의 대답	No, you may not[can't]. 아니, 그렇게 못해. I'm sorry, but you may not[can't]. 미안하지만, 안 된단다.

Check and Write

다음 빈칸에 들어갈 적절한 단어를 보기에서 골라 써 보세요.

1. 보기 sleeps slept sleep

May I [sleep] now?

저 이제 자도 돼요?

2. 보기 may may not

Yes, you [ ].

그래, 그러렴.

3. 보기 may may not

It [ ] be a dog!

그것은 개가 아닐지도 몰라!

4. 보기 May May not

[ ] I eat that ice cream?

저 아이스크림 먹어도 돼요?

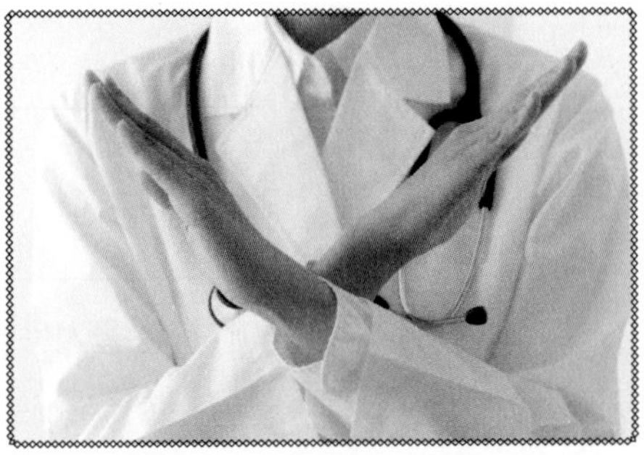

5. 보기 may may not

No, you [ ].

아니, 너는 그럴 수 없단다.

정답과 해설 p.2

Practice 1 조동사 can과 may의 알맞은 쓰임을 익혀 보아요.

주어진 우리말 뜻을 참고하여 보기에서 알맞은 말을 골라 빈칸에 써 보세요. (중복 사용 가능)

A Superheroes

보기 can cannot may

1. He __may__ be a superhero. 그는 슈퍼히어로일지도 몰라.

2. Spiderman ________ shoot webs from his hands.
   스파이더맨은 그의 손에서 거미줄을 쏠 수 있어.

3. Spiderman jumps high but ________ fly.
   스파이더맨은 높게 뛰지만 날 수는 없어.

4. Wolverine ________ heal very fast. (*heal: 낫다)
   울버린은 매우 빨리 나을 수 있어.

5. Iron Man ________ have superpowers without his suit.
   아이언맨은 그의 옷 없이는 초능력을 가질 수 없어. (*superpower: 초능력)

B In the classroom

보기 May[may] may not cannot

1. You ________ wear outdoor shoes in the classroom.
   교실에서는 실외화를 신을 수 없습니다.

2. ________ I go to the restroom? 화장실 가도 될까요?

3. You ________ have a seat. 자리에 앉아도 좋아요.

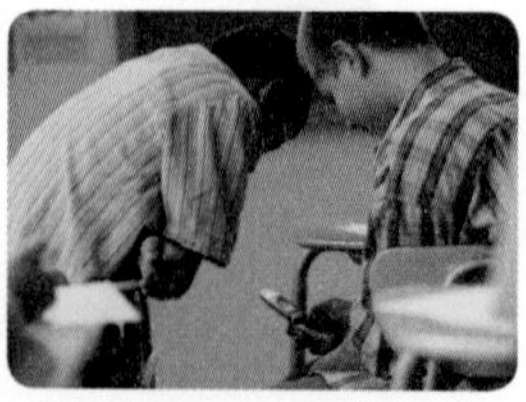

4. You ________ use your cell phone during class.
   수업 중에 휴대폰을 사용할 수 없습니다.

정답과 해설 p.2

5. Students __________ leave the classroom during the break.
학생들은 쉬는 시간에 교실을 떠나도 괜찮습니다.

6. This __________ be the right answer. 이게 맞는 답이 아닐지도 몰라.

C Gossip

보기 Can[can] cannot may not

1. __________ you keep a secret? 너 비밀 지킬 수 있어?

2. Of course. You __________ tell me anything.
물론이지. 나한테 뭐든지 말해도 돼.

3. Jihee __________ pass the exam. 지희가 시험을 통과하지 못할지도 몰라.

4. I __________ believe that! 난 그걸 믿을 수가 없어!

D Mom and I

보기 Can[can] can't may may not

1. __________ you do the dishes? 설거지 해 줄 수 있니?

2. No, I __________. I am busy. 아뇨, 못 해요. 나 바빠요.

3. Mom __________ tell if I lie. (*tell: 알다)
엄마는 내가 거짓말을 하는지 안 하는지를 아실 수 있다.

4. Mom __________ give me pocket money.
엄마가 나에게 용돈을 안 주실지도 몰라.

5. Mom __________ order pizza for dinner.
엄마가 저녁으로 피자를 주문하실지도 몰라.

정답과 해설 p.2

Practice 2 조동사 can과 may를 써서 문장을 완성해 보아요.

다음 우리말 뜻과 같도록 주어진 표현을 순서에 맞게 배열하여 문장을 완성하세요.

1. (can, I, a hamburger, eat) in two bites.
나는 햄버거 하나를 두 입에 먹을 수 있어.

➔ I can eat a hamburger in two bites.

2. My little sister (play, can, the piano).
내 여동생은 피아노를 연주할 수 있어.

➔ My little sister ______________________.

3. (swim, I, can). 난 수영할 수 있어.
➔ ______________________________________.

4. Yujin (not, come to school, may) because he hurt his leg.
다리를 다쳐서 유진이는 학교에 안 올지도 몰라.
➔ Yujin ______________________ because he hurt his leg.

5. Oh, no! Then, (can't, he, play the game) with us.
오, 저런! 그럼, 그는 우리와 함께 경기를 할 수 없잖아.
➔ Oh, no! Then, ______________________ with us.

6. (rain, may, It) tomorrow. 내일 비가 올지도 몰라.
➔ ______________________ tomorrow.

정답과 해설 p.2

7. So, (may, be cancelled, the soccer game). 그래서 축구 시합이 취소될지도 몰라.

→ So, ______________________________.

8. (change, my life, I, can). 나는 내 삶을 바꿀 수 있다.

→ ______________________________.

9. (I, play video games, may) all day tomorrow.
내일 하루 종일 난 비디오 게임을 할지도 모르겠네.

→ ______________________ all day tomorrow.

10. (may, be handsome, He), but he is mean. (*mean: 못된, 심술궂은)
그는 잘생겼을지는 모르지만, 못됐어.

→ ______________________, but he is mean.

11. (I, try on, May) this dress? Do you have a small size?
제가 이 드레스를 입어 봐도 될까요? 작은 사이즈 있어요?

→ ______________________ this dress? Do you have a small size?

12. We don't have it right now, but (can, we, order it).
지금은 없어요, 하지만 저희가 주문해 드릴 수 있어요.

→ We don't have it right now, but ______________________.

13. I like Jake. (be smart, He, may, not), but he is kind.
난 Jake가 좋아. 그는 똑똑하지 않을지는 모르지만, 친절해.

→ I like Jake. ______________________, but he is kind.

정답과 해설 p.2

14. (may, He, like, Somi). 그는 소미를 좋아할지도 몰라.

➜ ____.

15. (can't, I, it, believe). 난 그것을 믿을 수 없어.

➜ ____.

16. (I, speak, Can) to Jake, please? Jake와 통화할 수 있을까요?

➜ ____________________ to Jake, please?

17. (you, I, help, can). 난 너를 도와줄 수 있어.

➜ ____________________

____________________.

18. (may not, Your story, have) a happy ending.
네 이야기는 행복한 결말을 가지고 있지 않을 수도 있어.

➜ ______________________________ a happy ending.

19. (change the world, Your voice, can). 여러분의 목소리가(의견이) 세상을 바꿀 수 있습니다.

➜ ____.

20. (come true, can, Our dreams). 우리의 꿈들은 실현될 수 있다.

➜ ____.

정답과 해설 p.2

Practice 3 조동사 can과 may를 써서 문장을 완성해 보아요.

우리말 뜻을 참고하여 주어진 영어 표현을 사용해 문장을 완성해 보세요.

1. (ride a horse)
난 말을 탈 수 있어.

→ I can ride a horse
______________.

2. (Some sharks, live)
어떤 상어들은 민물에서 살 수 있다.

→ ______________
in fresh water.

3. (ride a bicycle) 너 자전거 탈 수 있어?
→ ______________?

4. (Clair, read Korean) Clair는 한국어를 읽지 못해.
→ ______________.

5. (understand) 그녀는 몇몇 한국어 단어를 이해할 수 있어.
→ ______________ some Korean words.

6. (understand English) 그녀는 영어를 이해할 수 있니?
→ ______________?

7. (take a picture) 제가 사진을 찍어도 될까요?
→ ______________?

8. (type Korean) 난 이 컴퓨터에서 한국어 타자를 칠 수 없어. (*type: 타자 치다)
→ ______________ on this computer.

9. (Usain Bolt, run) 우사인 볼트는 100미터를 10초 안에 뛸 수 있다.
→ ______________ 100 meters in 10 seconds.

정답과 해설 p.2

10. (use)

넌 내 노트북을 사용해도 좋아.

➔ ______________________ my notebook computer.

11. (go to the bathroom)

넌 화장실에 가도 좋아.

➔ ______________________ ______________________.

12. (sit here) 당신은 여기 앉아도 돼요.

➔ ____.

13. (LG, win) 이번 시즌엔 LG가 이길지도 몰라.

➔ ______________________________ this season.

14. (LG, beat, Doosan) 아니야, LG는 두산을 이길 수 없어. (*beat: 이기다)

➔ No, ______________________________.

15. (snow) 곧 눈이 올지도 몰라.

➔ ______________________________ soon.

16. (feel) 난 내 발을 느낄 수 없어.(난 발에 감각이 없어.)

➔ ______________________________ my feet.

17. (stay at our house) 넌 우리 집에 있어도 좋아.

➔ ____.

18. (watch TV) 너는 TV를 볼 수 없어.

➔ ______________________________.

19. (use the computer) 나는 컴퓨터를 사용할 수 없어.

➔ ____.

정답과 해설 p.2

Let's Practice More!

SET 01

학습목표 1 | 조동사의 여러 가지 특징을 익혀 보아요. 공부한 날 : 맞은 개수 : /12개

다음 ( ) 안에서 알맞은 것을 고르세요.

01. She may (be / is) a superhero.
그녀는 슈퍼히어로일지도 몰라.

02. Wolverine can (heal / heals) very fast.
울버린은 매우 빨리 나을 수 있어.

03. Jihee may not (pass / passes) the exam.
지희가 시험을 통과하지 못할지도 몰라.

04. Mom may (order / orders) pizza for dinner.
엄마가 저녁으로 피자를 주문하실지도 몰라.

05. My little sister can (play / plays) the piano.
내 여동생은 피아노를 연주할 수 있어.

06. It may (rain / rains) tomorrow.
내일 비가 올지도 몰라.

07. He may (like / likes) Somi.
그는 소미를 좋아할지도 몰라.

08. Your voice can (change / changes) the world.
여러분의 목소리가(의견이) 세상을 바꿀 수 있습니다.

09. She can (understand / understands) some Korean words.
그녀는 몇몇 한국어 단어를 이해할 수 있어.

10. Usain Bolt can (run / runs) 100 meters in 10 seconds.
우사인 볼트는 100미터를 10초 안에 뛸 수 있다.

11. LG may (win / wins) this season.
이번 시즌엔 LG가 이길지도 몰라.

12. It may (snow / snows) soon.
곧 눈이 올지도 몰라.

정답과 해설 p.2

Let's Practice More!

SET 02

학습목표 1 | 조동사의 여러 가지 특징을 익혀 보아요. 공부한 날 : 맞은 개수 : /14개

밑줄 친 단어가 맞으면 ○표, 틀리면 고쳐 써 보세요.

01. Spiderman can shoot webs from his hands. → ○
스파이더맨은 손에서 거미줄을 쏠 수 있어.

02. He jumps high but cannot fly. → ______
그는 높게 뛰지만 날 수는 없어.

03. Iron Man cannot has superpowers without his suit. → ______
아이언맨은 그의 옷 없이는 초능력을 가질 수 없어.

04. You cannot use your cell phone during class. → ______
수업 중에 휴대폰을 사용할 수 없습니다.

05. Students may leaves the classroom during the break. → ______
학생들은 쉬는 시간에 교실을 떠나도 괜찮습니다.

06. Mom can tell if I lie. → ______
엄마는 내가 거짓말을 하는지 안 하는지를 아실 수 있다.

07. I can eats a hamburger in two bites. → ______
나는 햄버거 하나를 두 입에 먹을 수 있어.

08. I can swims. → ______
난 수영할 수 있어.

09. He can't play the game with us. → ______
그는 우리와 함께 경기를 할 수 없어.

10. It may rains tomorrow. → ______
내일 비가 올지도 몰라.

11. The soccer game may is cancelled. → ______
축구 시합이 취소될지도 몰라.

12. I can change my life. → ______
나는 내 삶을 바꿀 수 있어.

13. He may is handsome, but he is mean. → ______
그는 잘생겼을지는 모르지만, 못됐어.

14. Can we order it? → ______
저희가 그것을 주문할 수 있나요?

정답과 해설 p.2

Let's Practice More!

SET 03

학습목표 1 | 조동사의 여러 가지 특징을 익혀 보아요.   공부한 날 :   맞은 개수 :   /14개

다음 ( ) 안에서 알맞은 것을 고르세요.

01. I (can ride / ride can) a horse.
난 말을 탈 수 있어.

02. Some sharks (can live / live can) in fresh water.
어떤 상어들은 민물에서 살 수 있다.

03. Clair (read cannot / cannot read) Korean.
Clair는 한국어를 읽지 못해.

04. She (understand can / can understand) some Korean words.
그녀는 몇몇 한국어 단어를 이해할 수 있어.

05. I (type can't / can't type) Korean on this computer.
난 이 컴퓨터에서 한국어 타자를 칠 수 없어.

06. Usain Bolt (can run / run can) 100 meters in 10 seconds.
우사인 볼트는 100미터를 10초 안에 뛸 수 있다.

07. You (sit may / may sit) here.
당신은 여기 앉아도 돼요.

08. LG (can't beat / beat can't) Doosan.
LG는 두산을 이길 수 없어.

09. You (may stay / stay may) at our house.
너는 우리 집에 있어도 좋아.

10. I (use cannot / cannot use) the computer.
나는 컴퓨터를 사용할 수 없어.

11. You (may have / have may) a seat.
자리에 앉아도 좋아요.

12. Junwoo (not may / may not) pass the exam.
준우가 시험을 통과하지 못할지도 몰라.

13. Mom (may order / order may) pizza for dinner.
엄마가 저녁으로 피자를 주문하실지도 몰라.

14. I (can eat / eat can) a hamburger in two bites.
나는 햄버거 하나를 두 입에 먹을 수 있어.

정답과 해설 p.2

Let's Practice More!

SET 04

학습목표 2 | can과 may의 여러 가지 뜻을 구분해 봐요. 공부한 날 : 맞은 개수 : /12개

다음 문장을 읽고 밑줄 친 can의 뜻이 능력이면 '능'을, 허락이면 '허'를 쓰세요.

01. Spiderman can shoot webs from his hands. → 능
스파이더맨은 손에서 거미줄을 쏠 수 있어.

02. You can stay at our house. → ______
넌 우리 집에 있어도 좋아.

03. Can you keep a secret? → ______
너 비밀 지킬 수 있어?

04. Of course. You can tell me anything. → ______
물론이지. 나한테 뭐든지 말해도 돼.

05. Can you do the dishes? → ______
설거지 해 줄 수 있니?

06. Can I speak to Jake, please? → ______
Jake와 통화할 수 있을까요?

07. Your voice can change the world. → ______
여러분의 목소리가(의견이) 세상을 바꿀 수 있습니다.

08. Can I take a picture? → ______
제가 사진을 찍어도 될까요?

09. You can use my notebook computer. → ______
넌 내 노트북을 사용해도 좋아.

10. Wolverine can heal very fast. → ______
울버린은 매우 빨리 나을 수 있어.

11. You can go to the bathroom. → ______
넌 화장실에 가도 좋아.

12. You can be a pilot. → ______
너는 파일럿이 될 수 있어.

정답과 해설 p.2

Let's Practice More!

SET 05

학습목표 2 | can과 may의 여러 가지 뜻을 구분해 봐요. 공부한 날 : 맞은 개수 : /14개

다음 문장을 읽고 밑줄 친 may의 뜻이 추측이면 '추', 허락이면 '허'를 쓰세요.

01. Students may leave the classroom during the break. → 허
학생들은 쉬는 시간에 교실을 떠나도 괜찮습니다.

02. This may not be the right answer. → ______
이게 맞는 답이 아닐지도 몰라.

03. Yujin may not come to school because he hurt his leg. → ______
다리를 다쳐서 유진이는 학교에 안 올지도 몰라.

04. May I try on this dress? → ______
제가 이 드레스를 입어 봐도 될까요?

05. He may like Somi. → ______
그는 소미를 좋아할지도 몰라.

06. May I take a picture? → ______
제가 사진을 찍어도 될까요?

07. You may sit here. → ______
당신은 여기 앉아도 돼요.

08. It may rain soon. → ______
곧 비가 올지도 몰라.

09. She may be a superhero. → ______
그녀는 슈퍼히어로일지도 몰라.

10. You may have a seat. → ______
자리에 앉아도 좋아요

11. He may not be smart, but he is kind. → ______
그는 똑똑하지 않을지는 모르지만, 친절해.

12. Your story may not have a happy ending. → ______
네 이야기는 행복한 결말을 가지고 있지 않을 수도 있어.

13. You may use my notebook computer. → ______
넌 내 노트북을 사용해도 좋아.

14. LG may win this season. → ______
이번 시즌엔 LG가 이길지도 몰라.

정답과 해설 p.2

Let's Practice More!

SET 06

학습목표 3 | 조동사를 이용한 질문에 대답해 보아요. 공부한 날 : 맞은 개수 : /14개

다음 의문문에 대한 대답을 완성해 보세요.

01. May I go to the restroom?
저 화장실에 가도 될까요?

➔ No, you __may__ __not__.
아니, 안 된다.

02. Can you keep a secret?
너 비밀 지킬 수 있어?

➔ Yes, I ________.
그럼, 지킬 수 있지.

03. Can you do the dishes?
설거지 해 줄 수 있니?

➔ No, I ________.
아니, 안 돼.

04. May I try on this dress?
제가 이 드레스를 입어 봐도 될까요?

➔ No, you ________ ________.
아니요, 안 됩니다.

05. Can I speak to Jake, please?
Jake와 통화할 수 있을까요?

➔ Yes, you ________.
네, 됩니다.

06. Can you ride a bicycle?
너 자전거 탈 수 있어?

➔ Yes, I ________.
그럼, 탈 수 있지.

정답과 해설 p.3

07. Can she understand English?
그녀는 영어를 이해할 수 있니?

➔ No, she ___________.
아니, 이해할 수 없어.

08. Can Iron Man have superpowers without his suit?
아이언맨은 그의 옷 없이 초능력을 가질 수 있니?

➔ No, he ___________.
아니, 가질 수 없어.

09. Can you play the piano?
너 피아노 연주할 수 있어?

➔ Yes, I ___________.
그럼, 연주할 수 있지.

10. Can you help me?
너 나를 도와줄 수 있니?

➔ Yes, I ___________.
그럼, 도와줄 수 있지.

11. Can our dreams come true?
우리의 꿈들은 실현될 수 있니?

➔ Yes, they ___________.
그럼, 실현될 수 있지.

12. May I use your notebook computer?
내가 너의 노트북을 사용해도 되니?

➔ No, you ___________ ___________.
아니, 안 돼.

13. May I have a seat?
자리에 앉아도 될까요?

➔ No, you ___________ ___________.
아니요, 안 됩니다.

14. Can Clair read Korean?
Clair는 한국어를 읽을 수 있니?

➔ Yes, she ___________.
그럼, 읽을 수 있지.

정답과 해설 p.3

Let's Practice More!

SET 07

학습목표 4 | **조동사를 이용해 문장을 완성해 보아요.** 공부한 날 : 맞은 개수 : /20개

( ) 안의 표현을 이용해 문장을 완성해 보세요. (단, 필요한 경우에 조동사를 부정형으로 바꿔 쓰세요.)

01.

I __may__ __play__ video games all day tomorrow. (may, play)

내일 하루 종일 난 비디오 게임을 할지도 모르겠네.

02.

I ________ ________ that! (can, believe)

난 그것을 믿을 수가 없어!

03. He jumps high but ________ ________. (can, fly) 그는 높게 뛰지만 날 수는 없어.

04. You ________ ________ outdoor shoes in the classroom. (can, wear)

교실에서 실외화를 신을 수 없습니다.

05. This ________ ________ ________ the right answer. (may, be)

이게 맞는 답이 아닐지도 몰라.

06. Of course. You ________ ________ me anything. (can, tell)

물론이지. 나한테 뭐든지 말해도 돼.

07. Mom ________ ________ ________ me pocket money. (may, give)

엄마가 나에게 용돈을 안 주실지도 몰라.

08. Yujin ________ ________ ________ to school because he hurt his leg. (may, come)

다리를 다쳐서 유진이는 학교에 안 올지도 몰라.

정답과 해설 p.3

09. I __________ __________ Korean on this computer. (can, type)
난 이 컴퓨터에서 한국어 타자를 칠 수 없어.

10. I __________ __________ my feet. (can, feel)
난 내 발을 느낄 수 없어.(난 발에 감각이 없어.)

11. You __________ __________ TV. (can, watch) 너는 TV를 볼 수 없어.

12. You __________ __________ your cell phone during class. (can, use)
수업 중에 휴대폰을 사용할 수 없습니다.

13. Mom __________ __________ if I lie. (can, tell)
엄마는 내가 거짓말을 하는지 안 하는지를 아실 수 있다.

14. He __________ __________ handsome, but he is mean.
(may, be) 그는 잘생겼을지는 모르지만, 못됐어.

15. We __________ __________ it. (can, order) 저희가 그것을 주문할 수 있어요.

16. I __________ __________ you. (can, help) 난 너를 도와줄 수 있어.

17. Your story __________ __________ __________ a happy ending. (may, have)
네 이야기는 행복한 결말을 가지고 있지 않을 수도 있어.

18. I __________ __________ a horse. (can, ride) 난 말을 탈 수 있어.

19. Some sharks __________ __________ in fresh water. (can, live)
어떤 상어들은 민물에서 살 수 있다.

20. LG __________ __________ Doosan. (can, beat) LG는 두산을 이길 수 없어.

정답과 해설 p.3

Let's Practice More!

SET 08

학습목표 4 | 조동사를 이용해 문장을 완성해 보아요.　　공부한 날 :　　맞은 개수 :　　/20개

( ) 안의 지시에 따라 문장을 바꿔 보세요.

01. You can wear outdoor shoes in the classroom. (의문문)

➔ Can you wear outdoor shoes in the classroom ?

너는 교실에서 실외화를 신을 수 있니?

02. I can believe that! (부정문)

➔ ______________________________!

나는 그것을 믿을 수가 없어!

03. Mom may give me pocket money. (부정문)

➔ ______________________________.

엄마가 나에게 용돈을 안 주실지도 몰라.

04. You can swim. (의문문)

➔ ______________________________?

너는 수영할 수 있니?

05. He can't play the game with us. (의문문)

➔ ______________________________?

그는 우리와 함께 경기를 할 수 없니?

06. The soccer game may be cancelled. (부정문)

➔ ______________________________.

그 축구 시합이 취소되지 않을지도 몰라.

07. I can change my life. (의문문)

➔ ______________________________?

내가 내 삶을 바꿀 수 있을까?

08. He can ride a bicycle. (부정문)

➔ ______________________________.

그는 자전거를 탈 수 없어.

09. Clair can read Korean. (부정문)

➔ ______________________________.

Clair는 한국어를 읽지 못해.

정답과 해설 p.3

10. She can understand English. (의문문)

➔ ____?

그녀는 영어를 이해할 수 있니?

11. You may go to the bathroom. (부정문)

➔ ____.

넌 화장실에 가면 안 돼.

12. I can feel my feet. (부정문)

➔ ____.

난 내 발을 느낄 수 없어.(난 발에 감각이 없어.)

13. You can watch TV. (의문문)

➔ ____?

너는 TV를 볼 수 있니?

14. I can use the computer. (부정문)

➔ ____.

나는 컴퓨터를 사용할 수 없어.

15. You can be a pilot. (의문문)

➔ ______________________________________?

너는 파일럿이 될 수 있니?

16. Iron Man can't have superpowers without his suit. (의문문)

➔ ____?

아이언맨은 그의 옷 없이 초능력을 가질 수 없니?

17. You may have a seat. (부정문)

➔ ____.

너는 자리에 앉으면 안 돼.

18. I can use my cell phone during class. (부정문)

➔ ______________________________________.

나는 수업시간에 핸드폰을 쓸 수 없어.

19. I can keep a secret. (부정문)

➔ ____.

나는 비밀을 지킬 수 없어.

20. Yujin may come to school. (부정문)

➔ ____.

유진이는 학교에 안 올지도 몰라.

정답과 해설 p.3

UNIT

03 You must[have to] choose.

조동사 must, have to (1)

❖ POiNT 1 ❖

must / have to[has to]는 '~해야 한다'라는 의미의 조동사예요.
반드시 뒤에 동사원형이 온다는 사실 기억하고 있겠죠?

의무	must	You **must** choose. 너는 선택을 해야 해. We **must** arrive on time. 우리는 제시간에 도착해야 해. She **must** do her homework! 그녀는 그녀의 숙제를 해야 해!
	have to [has to]	I **have to** draw a picture. 나는 그림을 그려야만 해. I **have to** see a doctor. I am sick. 나는 병원에 가야 해. 나 아파. He **has to** wear a coat. It's cold. 그는 코트를 입어야 해. 날씨가 추워.

❖ POiNT 2 ❖

must와 달리 have to는 시제와 주어에 따라 모양이 변해요.
또, 예외적으로 have to는 다른 조동사와 함께 쓰일 수 있답니다.

	현재 (~해야 한다)	과거 (~해야 했다)	미래 (~해야 할 것이다)
She, He, It	has to	had to	will have to
I, You, We, They	have to		

Check and Write

다음 빈칸에 들어갈 적절한 표현을 보기에서 골라 써 보세요.

1. 보기 has to must had to

I [must] go now.
나는 지금 가야 해.

2. 보기 have to must had to

He [   ] do his homework now.
그는 지금 그의 숙제를 해야 해.

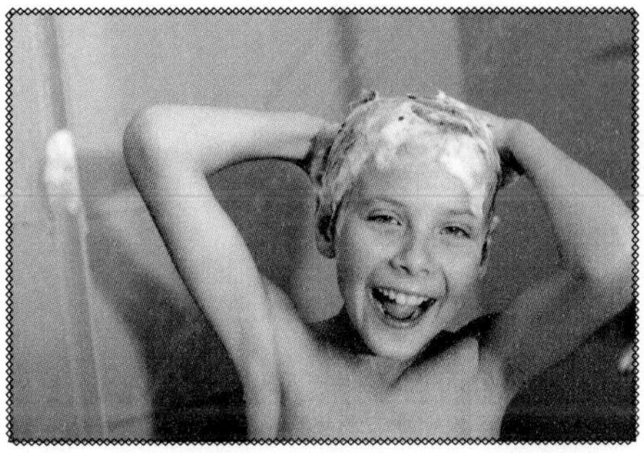

3. 보기 have to has to had to

You [   ] wash your hair.
너는 머리를 감아야 해.

4. 보기 have to has to had to

She [   ] clean her room yesterday.
그녀는 어제 방 청소를 해야 했어.

5. 보기 has to must had to

You [   ] get up early.
너는 일찍 일어나야 해.

정답과 해설 p.3

UNIT 조동사 must, have to (2)

04 We must not tell lies.

❖ POiNT 1 ❖

must와 have to는 의미가 거의 같지만, 부정문을 만들면 의미가 달라져요!

must not + 동사원형 ~ 해서는 안 된다	You **must not** run near the pool. 너는 수영장 근처에서 뛰면 **안 된다**.  We **must not** tell lies. 우리는 거짓말을 하면 **안 된다**.
don't[doesn't] have to + 동사원형 ~ 할 필요가 없다	We **don't have to** go to school this Wednesday. It's a holiday! 우리는 이번 주 수요일에 학교에 갈 **필요 없어**. 휴일이잖아! You **don't have to** worry. 넌 걱정할 **필요 없어**. She **doesn't have to** wear a jacket. It is warm today. 그녀는 재킷을 입을 **필요 없어**. 오늘 따뜻하거든. I **don't have to** do my homework today. 난 오늘 내 숙제를 할 **필요 없어**.

❖ POiNT 2 ❖

don't[doesn't] have to의 과거형 : didn't have to ~할 필요가 없었다

I **didn't have to** buy new shoes.
난 새 신발을 살 **필요가 없었어**.

Check and Write

다음 빈칸에 들어갈 적절한 표현을 보기에서 골라 써 보세요.

1. 보기 don't have to must not

You [must not] touch it.
너는 그것을 만지면 안 돼.

2. 보기 don't have to must not

We [ ] waste water.
우리는 물을 낭비해서는 안 된다.

3. 보기 doesn't have to must not

She [ ] clean the kitchen.
그녀는 부엌을 청소하지 않아도 돼.

4. 보기 doesn't have to don't have to

You [ ] worry.
너는 걱정할 필요가 없어.

5. 보기 must not don't have to

We [ ] bother the animals.
우리는 동물들을 귀찮게 해선 안 된다.

정답과 해설 p.3

Practice 1 조동사 must와 have to의 알맞은 쓰임을 익혀 보아요.

주어진 우리말 뜻을 참고하여 보기에서 알맞은 표현을 골라 빈칸에 써 보세요. (중복 사용 가능)

A Traffic rules

보기 must must not have to

1. You are sleepy. You must not drive a car.
당신은 졸려요. 당신은 운전하면 안 됩니다.

2. You __________ cross this line. 이 선을 넘으면 안 됩니다.

3. You __________ pay for parking. (*parking: 주차)
주차하려면 돈을 내야 합니다.

4. You __________ turn left here. 여기서 좌회전하시면 안 됩니다.

5. You __________ be careful. It's a school zone.
조심해야 합니다. 여기는 어린이 보호구역입니다.

B Beach vacation

보기 must must not have to

1. We don't __________ pay. 우리는 돈을 내지 않아도 돼.

2. We __________ pay for the beach umbrellas and chairs.
우리는 비치파라솔과 의자는 돈을 내야 해.

3. You __________ swim out too far. 넌 너무 멀리까지 수영하면 안 된다.

4. You __________ put on sunblock. 넌 자외선 차단제를 발라야 해.

정답과 해설 p.3

C Final exam week

보기 must have to has to had to

1. You ________ read the textbooks. 넌 교과서를 읽어야 해.

2. Jisun ________ study for the math exam.
지선이는 수학 시험을 위해 공부해야 한다.

3. Minji ________ borrow my notes. 민지는 내 노트를 빌려야 했어.

4. You will ________ get a B. 너는 B를 받아야 할 것이다.

5. I ________ go to the library. 난 도서관에 가야 해.

D Eating out

보기 have to must must not

1. We ________ wait for the dinner. 우리는 저녁식사를 기다려야 해.

2. We don't ________ order dessert. 우리는 디저트를 주문하지 않아도 돼.

3. You ________ try the cheese pizza at this restaurant. (*try: ~해 보다)
이 음식점에서 치즈 피자는 꼭 먹어 봐야 해.

4. We ________ leave food on our plates.
우리는 음식을 남기면 안 돼.

정답과 해설 p.3

Practice 2 조동사 must와 have to를 써서 문장을 완성해 보아요.

다음 우리말 뜻과 같도록 주어진 표현을 순서에 맞게 배열하여 문장을 완성하세요.

1. (don't have to, You, go). It's only 4 o'clock.
너는 갈 필요 없어. 겨우 4시인걸.

→ You don't have to go. It's only 4 o'clock.

2. (eat dinner, I, Do, have to)? I am not hungry.
저 저녁 먹어야 해요? 전 배 안 고파요.

→ ________________? I am not hungry.

3. (I, go home, have to). 나 집에 가야 해.

→ ________________.

4. (have to, have dinner, I) with my family. 나는 가족들과 함께 저녁을 먹어야 하거든.

→ ________________ with my family.

5. (call my mom, have to, I). 나 엄마한테 전화해야 해.

→ ________________.

6. (must not, You, skip meals). 식사를 거르면 안 된다.

→ ________________.

7. (have to, Do, I, wear pants)? 저 바지 입어야 해요?

→ ________________?

8. (must, follow the rules, You). 넌 규칙을 따라야만 해.

→ ________________.

정답과 해설 p.3

9. (has to, Andy, clean his room). Andy는 방을 청소해야 해.

➔ ________________________.

10. (You, have to, worry, don't). 너는 걱정할 필요 없어.

➔ ________________________.

11. (change the rules, must, They)! 그들은 규칙을 바꿔야만 해요!

➔ ____!

12. (take care of, has to, He) his sister. 그는 그의 여동생을 돌봐야 해.

➔ ________________________ his sister.

13. (don't have to, be mean, We) to him. 우리가 그에게 나쁘게 대할 필요는 없잖아.

➔ ________________________ to him.

14. (have to, be a snowman, It, doesn't). 그게 눈사람이 아니어도 돼.

➔ ____.

15. (He, change his clothes, has to). 그는 옷을 갈아입어야만 해.

➔ ____.

16. (must, You, try) many times. 너는 여러 번 시도해야 해.

➔ ________________________ many times.

17. (forget, We, must) bad things. 우리는 나쁜 것들을 잊어야 해.

➔ ________________________ bad things.

18. (You, save power, must). 너는 힘을 아껴야 해.

➔ ____.

정답과 해설 p.3

Practice 3 조동사 must와 have to를 써서 문장을 완성해 보아요.

우리말 뜻을 참고하여 다음 주어진 표현을 사용해 문장을 완성해 보세요.

1. (have to, water this plant)
나는 이 식물에 물을 줘야 한다.

→ I have to water this plant.

2. (have to, do my homework)
나는 컴퓨터로 숙제를 해야 해.

→ ______________________ on a computer.

3. (have to, plant trees) 당신은 나무를 심어야 합니다.
→ ______________________.

4. (has to, drink milk) 그녀는 우유를 마셔야 합니다.
→ ______________________.

5. (must, look at, the sun) 넌 태양을 직접 보면 안 돼. (*directly: 직접적으로)
→ ______________________ directly.

6. (must, wear sunglasses) 넌 선글라스를 껴야만 해.
→ ______________________.

7. (have to, remember his name) 난 그의 이름을 기억해야만 해.
→ ______________________.

8. (Dad, has to, go) 아빠는 내일 중국에 가셔야 해.
→ ______________________ to China tomorrow.

정답과 해설 p.3

9. (must, use a pencil)
여러분은 답안지에 연필을 사용하셔야 합니다.

➔ ____________________ on the answer sheet.

10. (have to, raise your hand)
여러분은 질문하려면 손을 들어야 합니다.

➔ ____________________ to ask questions.

11. (must, forget his passport) (*passport: 여권) 그는 그의 여권을 잊어서는 안 되겠네요.

➔ ______________________________.

12. (have to, worry) 너는 그것에 대해 걱정할 필요는 없단다.

➔ ______________________________ about that.

13. (must, bring) 그는 저에게 선물을 가져와야만 해요!

➔ ______________________________ me a gift!

14. (must, stop) 여러분은 여기에서 멈춰야 합니다.

➔ ______________________________ here.

15. (My parents, must, buy) 우리 부모님은 나에게 새 컴퓨터를 사주셔야만 해.

➔ ______________________________ me a new computer.

16. (It, have to, be) 그것이 비싼 모델일 필요는 없어. (*expensive: 비싼)

➔ ______________________________ an expensive model.

17. (My computer, must, have) 내 컴퓨터는 큰 화면을 가지고 있어야만 해.

➔ ______________________________ a big screen.

18. (have to, visit) 넌 컴퓨터 상점을 방문해야 해.

➔ ______________________________ the computer store.

19. (must, buy computers) 넌 컴퓨터를 온라인에서 사면 안 돼.

➔ ______________________________ online.

정답과 해설 p.4

Let's Practice More!

SET 01

학습목표 1 | must와 have to의 여러 가지 특징을 익혀 보아요. 공부한 날 : 맞은 개수 : /12개

다음 ( ) 안에서 알맞은 것을 고르세요.

01. You must not (drive / drove) a car.
당신은 운전하면 안 됩니다.

02. You have to (pay / paid) for parking.
주차하려면 돈을 내야 합니다.

03. You must not (turned / turn) left here.
여기서 좌회전하시면 안 됩니다.

04. We have to (pay / paid) for the beach umbrellas and chairs.
우리는 비치파라솔과 의자에 돈을 내야 해.

05. You must not (swam / swim) out too far.
넌 너무 멀리까지 수영하면 안 된다.

06. Jisun has to (studied / study) for the math exam.
지선이는 수학 시험을 위해 공부해야 한다.

07. Minji had to (borrow / borrowed) my notes.
민지는 내 노트를 빌려야 했어.

08. I must (went / go) to the library.
난 도서관에 가야 해.

09. I have to (have / had) dinner with my family.
나는 가족들과 함께 저녁을 먹어야 해.

10. I have to (called / call) my mom.
나 엄마한테 전화해야 해.

11. They must (change / changed) the rules!
그들은 규칙을 바꿔야만 해요!

12. She has to (took / take) care of her sister.
그녀는 그녀의 여동생을 돌봐야 해.

정답과 해설 p.4

Let's Practice More!

SET 02

학습목표 1 | must와 have to의 여러 가지 특징을 익혀 보아요. 공부한 날 : 맞은 개수 : /14개

밑줄 친 단어가 맞으면 ○표, 틀리면 고쳐 써 보세요.

01. I has to go home. → have
나 집에 가야 해.

02. You musts not skip meals. → ______
식사를 거르면 안 된다.

03. Andy has to clean his room. → ______
Andy는 방을 청소해야 해.

04. You doesn't have to worry. → ______
너는 걱정할 필요 없어.

05. He has to take care of his sister. → ______
그는 그의 여동생을 돌봐야 해.

06. You must try many times. → ______
너는 여러 번 시도해야 해.

07. He have to change his clothes. → ______
그는 옷을 갈아입어야만 해.

08. I has to water this plant. → ______
나는 이 식물에 물을 줘야 한다.

09. You have to visit the computer store. → ______
넌 컴퓨터 상점을 방문해야 해.

10. You must not look at the sun directly. → ______
넌 태양을 직접 보면 안 돼.

11. Dad has to go to China tomorrow. → ______
아빠는 내일 중국에 가셔야 해.

12. He musts bring me a gift! → ______
그는 저에게 선물을 가져와야만 해요!

13. You must stop here. → ______
여러분은 여기에서 멈춰야 합니다.

14. It doesn't have to be an expensive model. → ______
그것이 비싼 모델일 필요는 없어.

정답과 해설 p.4

Let's Practice More!

SET 03

학습목표 1 | must와 have to의 여러 가지 특징을 익혀 보아요. 공부한 날 : 맞은 개수 : /14개

다음 ( ) 안에서 알맞은 것을 고르세요.

01. My parents (must buy / buy must) me a new computer.
우리 부모님은 나에게 새 컴퓨터를 사주셔야만 해.

02. My computer (must have / have must) a big screen.
내 컴퓨터는 큰 화면을 가지고 있어야만 해.

03. You (has to / have to) visit the computer store.
넌 컴퓨터 상점을 방문해야 해.

04. She (has to / have to) wear a coat.
그녀는 코트를 입어야 해.

05. You (be must / must be) careful.
넌 조심해야 해.

06. We don't (have to pay / pay have to).
우리는 돈을 내지 않아도 돼.

07. You (have to / has to) put on sunblock.
넌 자외선 차단제를 발라야 해.

08. You will (get have to / have to get) a B.
너는 B를 받아야 할 것이다.

09. We (has to / have to) wait for the dinner.
우리는 저녁식사를 기다려야 해.

10. Do I (have to eat / eat have to) dinner?
저 저녁 먹어야 해요?

11. Andy (have to / has to) clean his room.
Andy는 방을 청소해야 해.

12. It (doesn't have to / don't have to) be a snowman.
그게 눈사람이 아니어도 돼.

13. You (save must / must save) power.
너는 힘을 아껴야 해.

14. She (has to / have to) drink milk.
그녀는 우유를 마셔야 합니다.

정답과 해설 p.4

Let's Practice More!

SET 04

학습목표 2 | must와 have to의 부정형을 익혀 보아요. 공부한 날 : 맞은 개수 : /12개

다음 우리말 해석에 맞게 빈칸에 must 또는 have to의 부정형을 써 보세요.

01. We ___don't have to___ be mean to him.
우리는 그에게 나쁘게 대할 필요는 없잖아.

02. It ________________ be a snowman.
그게 눈사람이 아니어도 돼.

03. You ________________ look at the sun directly.
넌 태양을 직접 보면 안 돼.

04. He ________________ forget his passport.
그는 그의 여권을 잊어서는 안 돼.

05. You ________________ worry about that.
너는 그것에 대해 걱정할 필요는 없단다.

06. It ________________ be an expensive model.
그것이 비싼 모델일 필요는 없어.

07. You ________________ buy computers online.
넌 컴퓨터를 온라인에서 사면 안 돼.

08. We ________________ tell lies.
우리는 거짓말을 하면 안 된다.

09. They ________________ worry.
그들은 걱정 할 필요 없어.

10. You ________________ drive a car.
당신은 운전하면 안 됩니다.

11. You ________________ cross this line.
이 선을 넘으면 안 됩니다.

12. We ________________ pay.
우리는 돈을 내지 않아도 돼.

정답과 해설 p.4

Let's Practice More!

SET 05

학습목표 2 | must와 have to의 부정형을 익혀 보아요. 공부한 날 : 맞은 개수 : /14개

다음 문장을 읽고 밑줄 친 부분이 맞으면 ○표, 틀리면 고쳐 쓰세요.

01. You must not turns left here. → must not turn
여기서 좌회전하시면 안 됩니다.

02. You doesn't have to try the cheese pizza at this restaurant. → ____________
넌 이 식당에서 치즈 피자를 먹어 보지 않아도 돼.

03. We must not leave food on our plates. → ____________
우리는 음식을 남기면 안 돼.

04. You don't have to go now. → ____________
너는 지금 갈 필요 없어.

05. You must not wear sunglasses. → ____________
넌 선글라스를 끼면 안 돼.

06. We don't have to order dessert. → ____________
우리는 디저트를 주문하지 않아도 돼.

07. You must not swims out too far. → ____________
넌 너무 멀리까지 수영하면 안 된다.

08. You don't have to worry. → ____________
너는 걱정할 필요 없어.

09. They doesn't have to change the rules! → ____________
그들은 규칙을 바꿀 필요가 없어요!

10. We doesn't have to be mean to him. → ____________
우리가 그에게 나쁘게 대할 필요는 없잖아.

11. You don't have to change your clothes. → ____________
너는 옷을 갈아입지 않아도 돼.

12. Dad don't have to go to China tomorrow. → ____________
아빠는 내일 중국에 가지 않으셔도 돼.

13. He must not forget his passport. → ____________
그는 그의 여권을 잊어서는 안돼.

14. She don't have to wear a coat. → ____________
그녀는 코트를 입지 않아도 돼.

정답과 해설 p.4

Let's Practice More!

SET 06

학습목표 3 | must와 have to를 이용해 문장을 완성해 보아요. 　공부한 날 : 　맞은 개수 : 　/14개

( ) 안의 표현들을 이용해 문장을 완성해 보세요.

01.

You ___have___ ___to___ ___raise___ your hand to ask questions. (have to, raise)

여러분은 질문하려면 손을 들어야 합니다.

02.

You __________ __________ __________ early. (must, get up)

너는 일찍 일어나야 해.

03. I __________ __________ __________ his name. (have to, remember)

난 그의 이름을 기억해야만 해.

04. You __________ __________ a pencil on the answer sheet. (must, use)

여러분은 답안지에 연필을 사용하셔야 합니다.

05. We __________ __________ on time. (must, arrive)

우리는 제시간에 도착해야 해.

06. Do I __________ __________ __________ pants? (have to, wear)

저 바지 입어야 해요?

07. You __________ __________ the rules. (must, follow)

넌 규칙을 따라야만 해.

정답과 해설 p.4

08. You __________ __________ many times.

(must, try)

너는 여러 번 시도해야 해.

09. I __________ __________ __________ my homework on a computer.

(have to, do)

나는 컴퓨터로 숙제를 해야 해.

10. You __________ __________ __________ this line.

(must, cross)

이 선을 넘으면 안 됩니다.

11. You __________ __________ __________ for parking.

(have to, pay)

주차하려면 돈을 내야 합니다.

12. Jisun __________ __________ for the math exam.

(must, study)

지선이는 수학 시험을 위해 공부해야 한다.

13. Minji __________ __________ __________ my notes.

(had to, borrow)

민지는 내 노트를 빌려야 했어.

14. We __________ __________ __________ food on our plates.

(must, leave)

우리는 음식을 남기면 안 돼.

정답과 해설 p.4

Let's Practice More!

SET 07

학습목표 3 | must와 have to를 이용해 문장을 완성해 보아요.　　공부한 날 :　　맞은 개수 :　　/20개

다음 문장을 (　) 안에 주어진 주어로 시작하는 문장으로 바꿔 보세요.

01. You have to be careful. (He) 조심해야 합니다.

→ He has to be careful.

02. We have to pay for the beach umbrellas and chairs. (Andy)
우리는 비치파라솔과 의자에 돈을 내야 해.

→ ______________________.

03. You have to put on sunblock. (She) 넌 자외선 차단제를 발라야 해.

→ ______________________.

04. You have to read the textbooks. (Jane) 넌 교과서를 읽어야 해.

→ ______________________.

05. I have to go to the library. (We) 난 도서관에 가야 해.

→ ______________________.

06. We have to wait for the dinner. (He) 우리는 저녁식사를 기다려야 해.

→ ______________________.

07. We don't have to order dessert. (Minji) 우리는 디저트를 주문하지 않아도 돼.

→ ______________________.

08. You have to try the cheese pizza at this restaurant. (She)
이 음식점에서 치즈 피자는 꼭 먹어 봐야 해.

→ ______________________.

09. You don't have to go. (He) 너는 갈 필요 없어.

→ ______________________.

정답과 해설 p.4

10. Do I have to eat dinner? (Jisun) 저 저녁 먹어야 해요?

➔ ____?

11. I have to go home. (She) 나 집에 가야 해.

➔ ____.

12. I have to have dinner with Jake. (He)
나는 Jake와 함께 저녁을 먹어야 해.

➔ ______________________________.

13. Do I have to wear pants? (Jisun) 저 바지 입어야 해요?

➔ ____?

14. You have to follow the rules. (My sister) 넌 규칙을 따라야만 해.

➔ ____.

15. You have to try many times. (She) 너는 여러 번 시도해야 해.

➔ ____.

16. We have to forget bad things. (You) 우리는 나쁜 것들을 잊어야 해.

➔ ____.

17. She has to drink milk. (We) 그녀는 우유를 마셔야 합니다.

➔ ____.

18. He has to bring me a gift!(They) 그는 저에게 선물을 가져오셔야만 해요!

➔ ____!

19. My parents have to buy me a new computer. (He)
우리 부모님은 나에게 새 컴퓨터를 사주셔야만 해.

➔ ____.

20. You must stop here. (She) 여러분은 여기에서 멈춰야 합니다.

➔ ____.

정답과 해설 p.4

Let's Practice More!

SET 08

학습목표 3 | must와 have to를 이용해 문장을 완성해 보아요. 공부한 날 : 맞은 개수 : /20개

( ) 안의 지시에 따라 문장의 시제를 바꿔 보세요.

01. I have to call my mom. (과거)

나 엄마한테 전화해야 해.

➔ I had to call my mom.

나 엄마한테 전화해야 했어.

02. You have to save power. (과거)

너는 힘을 아껴야 해.

➔ ______________________________.

너는 힘을 아껴야 했어.

03. I have to do my homework on a computer. (미래)

나는 컴퓨터로 숙제를 해야 해.

➔ ______________________________.

나는 컴퓨터로 숙제를 해야 할 거야.

04. You have to wear sunglasses. (미래)

넌 선글라스를 껴야만 해.

➔ ______________________________.

넌 선글라스를 껴야만 할 거야.

05. I have to remember his name. (과거)

난 그의 이름을 기억해야만 해.

➔ ______________________________.

난 그의 이름을 기억해야만 했어.

06. You have to use a pencil on the answer sheet. (과거)

여러분은 답안지에 연필을 사용하셔야 합니다.

➔ ______________________________.

여러분은 답안지에 연필을 사용하셨어야 합니다.

정답과 해설 p.4

07. You have to raise your hand to ask questions. (미래)
여러분은 질문하려면 손을 들어야 합니다.

➔ ____.
여러분은 질문하려면 손을 들어야 할 것입니다.

08. You have to visit the computer store. (미래)
넌 컴퓨터 상점을 방문해야 해.

➔ ____.
넌 컴퓨터 상점을 방문해야 할 거야.

09. You have to buy computers offline. (과거)
넌 컴퓨터를 오프라인에서 사야 해.

➔ ____.
넌 컴퓨터를 오프라인에서 사야 했어.

10. We have to arrive on time. (과거)
우리는 제시간에 도착해야 해.

➔ ____.
우리는 제시간에 도착해야 했어.

11. You have to get up early. (미래)
너는 일찍 일어나야 해.

➔ ______________________________.
너는 일찍 일어나야 할 거야.

12. They have to worry. (과거)
그들은 걱정해야 해.

➔ ____.
그들은 걱정해야 했어.

13. You have to get a B. (미래)
너는 B를 받아야 해.

➔ ____.
너는 B를 받아야 할 거야.

정답과 해설 p.5

14. He has to bring me a gift! (과거)
그는 저에게 선물을 가져와야만 해요!

➔ ____!
그는 저에게 선물을 가져와야만 했어요!

15. You have to stop here. (과거)
여러분은 여기에서 멈춰야 합니다.

➔ ____.
여러분은 여기에서 멈춰야 했습니다.

16. I have to water this plant. (미래)
나는 이 식물에 물을 줘야 해.

➔ ______________________________.
나는 이 식물에 물을 줘야 할 거야.

17. My computer has to have a big screen. (미래)
내 컴퓨터는 큰 화면을 가지고 있어야만 해.

➔ ____.
내 컴퓨터는 큰 화면을 가지고 있어야만 할 거야.

18. You have to pay for parking. (미래)
주차하려면 돈을 내야 합니다.

➔ ____.
주차하려면 돈을 내야 할 겁니다.

19. You have to be careful. (미래)
조심해야 합니다.

➔ ______________________________.
조심해야 할 것입니다.

20. You have to read the textbooks. (과거)
넌 교과서를 읽어야 해.

➔ ____.
넌 교과서를 읽어야 했어.

정답과 해설 p.5

Chapter 02 형용사

이 챕터에서는 사람이나 사물의 상태, 특징을
설명하는 말인 '형용사'에 대해 배워 보아요.

☆ 학습 방향 및 배울 내용 미리보기 ☆

- [ ] **Unit 01 :** I have a **yellow** umbrella.
  형용사의 종류와 역할 (1)
  다양한 의미를 나타내는 형용사의 종류에 대해 알아보아요.

▼

- [ ] **Unit 02 :** I like **warm** hugs.
  형용사의 종류와 역할 (2)
  형용사의 두 가지 역할에 대해 알아보아요.

단어 미리보기

이 챕터에 나올 단어들 중 이미 알고 있는 단어가 있나요?
맞는 뜻을 골라 체크해 봐요.

날짜 : 이름 : 알고 있는 단어의 수 : /24개

No.	아는 단어	단어	품사	알맞은 뜻에 체크 표시해 봐요.			
1	✔	famous	형용사	유명한	✔	이름 없는	☐
2	☐	salty	형용사	단	☐	짠	☐
3	☐	spicy	형용사	매운	☐	신	☐
4	☐	bitter	형용사	쓴	☐	싱거운	☐
5	☐	watermelon	명사	메론	☐	수박	☐
6	☐	soft	형용사	부드러운	☐	딱딱한	☐
7	☐	sweet	형용사	싱거운	☐	단	☐
8	☐	sound	동사	보이다	☐	~처럼 들리다	☐
9	☐	skirt	명사	스키	☐	치마	☐
10	☐	teenager	명사	10대	☐	초등학생	☐
11	☐	ant	명사	개미	☐	벌	☐
12	☐	important	형용사	중요한	☐	사소한	☐
13	☐	dirty	형용사	깨끗한	☐	더러운	☐
14	☐	ugly	형용사	잘생긴	☐	못생긴	☐
15	☐	brave	형용사	용감한	☐	겁 많은	☐
16	☐	fresh	형용사	상한	☐	신선한	☐
17	☐	write	동사	쓰다	☐	읽다	☐
18	☐	ready	형용사	준비가 된	☐	늦은	☐
19	☐	loyal	형용사	약한	☐	충성스러운	☐
20	☐	choice	명사	실수	☐	선택	☐
21	☐	full	형용사	배부른	☐	배고픈	☐
22	☐	taste	동사	맛보다	☐	느끼다	☐
23	☐	honest	형용사	욕심 많은	☐	정직한	☐
24	☐	difficult	형용사	다른	☐	어려운	☐

UNIT 01 I have a yellow umbrella.

❖ POiNT 1 ❖

형용사는 '배고픈, 예쁜, 큰'처럼 사람이나 사물의 상태, 특징을 설명하는 말이에요.

I	have	an umbrella.	
나는	가지고 있어	우산을	
I	have	a yellow	umbrella.
나는	가지고 있어	노란	우산을

❖ POiNT 2 ❖

형용사는 상태, 색깔, 크기, 날씨, 맛과 같은 것을 나타내요.

상태	 beautiful(아름다운)	 thirsty(목마른)	 cute(귀여운)	 famous(유명한)	
색깔	 black(검은)	 white(흰)	 blue(파란)	 red(빨간)	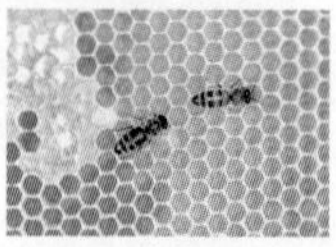 yellow(노란)
크기	 big(큰) small(작은)	 tall(키가 큰) short(키가 작은)			
날씨	 sunny(화창한)	 rainy(비 오는)	 cloudy(구름 낀)	 windy(바람 부는)	
맛	 sweet (달콤한)	 sour(신)	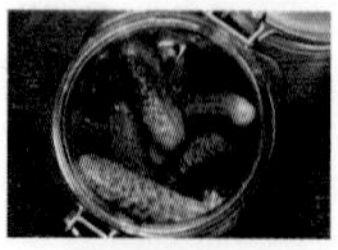 salty(짠)	 spicy, hot (매운)	 bitter(쓴)

Check and Write

다음 단어들 중에서 형용사를 모두 골라 동그라미 해보세요.

1. 

funny

2. 

watermelon

3. 

sick

4. 

dog

5. 

happy

6. 

green

7. 

strong

8. 

robot

9. 

warm

10. 

soft

11. 

smartphone

12. 

angry

정답과 해설 p.5

UNIT 02 I like warm hugs.

형용사의 종류와 역할 (2)

형용사는 두 가지 역할을 해요!

❖ POiNT 1 ❖

명사 수식

주로 **명사 앞에 놓여** 명사를 꾸며줘요.

I like **warm** hugs. 난 따뜻한 포옹을 좋아해.

I have an **early** dinner. 난 이른 저녁식사를 해.

I like **sweet** cotton candy.

나는 달콤한 솜사탕을 좋아해.

※something, anything, nothing 같은 단어는 형용사가 뒤에서 꾸며요!

I need something **hot**. 난 뜨거운 것이 필요해.

❖ POiNT 2 ❖

보어 역할

be동사와 짝이 되어 **주어의 상태를 설명**해요.

I am **thirsty**. Can I have a glass of water?

저 목말라요. 물 한 잔 마실 수 있나요?

Rabbit : Your legs are **short** and you are **slow**.

토끼 : 너의 다리는 짧고 넌 느려.

Tortoise : My legs may be **short**.
And I may be **slow**.
But I can beat you in a race.

거북이 : 내 다리는 짧을지도 몰라. 그리고 난 느릴지도 모르지.
하지만 난 널 경주에서 이길 수 있어.

[토끼와 거북이]

※형용사는 감각동사와도 짝이 될 수 있어요.

감각동사란 **look, smell, sound, taste, feel**처럼 보고 듣고 느끼는 동사를 의미해요.

You look **nice** in that skirt. 너 그 치마 입으니까 멋져 보여.

This pizza smells **good**. 이 피자는 맛있는 냄새가 나.

Check and Write

보기에서 적절한 형용사를 골라 빈칸에 넣어보세요.

보기 cold hungry shy sweet white sick

1. I like [cold] ice cream.
나는 차가운 아이스크림을 좋아해.

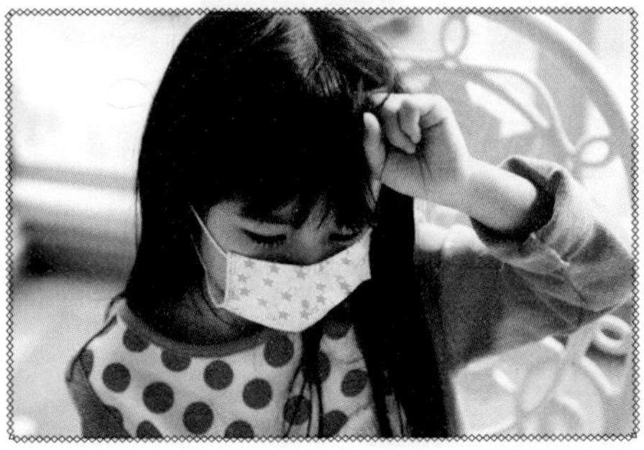

2. She feels [ ].
그녀는 아파.

3. You have [ ] shoes.
너는 흰 신발을 가지고 있구나.

4. He is [ ].
그는 배고파.

5. I want something [ ].
나는 달콤한 무언가를 원해.

6. She is very [ ].
그녀는 매우 수줍어해.

정답과 해설 p.5

Practice 1 상황에 맞는 적절한 형용사를 익혀 보아요.

다음 문장에 알맞은 표현을 보기에서 골라 빈칸에 써 보세요.

A I like it.

보기 pretty famous sour sweet

1. Do you like __sweet__ candy?
   넌 달콤한 사탕을 좋아해?

2. I like ________ jelly candy like Trolli.
   나는 트롤리 같은 신 젤리를 좋아해.

3. Lee Sumin is a ________ entertainer for teenagers. (*entertainer: 연예인)
   이수민은 10대들에게 유명한 연예인이야.

4. She is ________. 그녀는 예뻐.

B Various animals! (*various: 다양한)

보기 cute slow tiny fast smart

1. My dog is ________. 나의 개는 영리해.

2. Your cat is so ________. 너의 고양이는 너무 귀여워.

3. A cheetah is very ________.
   치타는 매우 빨라.

4. A tortoise is ________. 거북이는 느려.

5. An ant is ________. 개미는 작아.

정답과 해설 p.5

C How's the weather?

보기 sunny hot windy rainy humid

1. It is __________ today. 오늘 비 와.

2. It is too __________. (*humid: 습한)
   너무 습하다.

3. I don't like __________ days. 나는 바람이 많이 부는 날을 좋아하지 않아.

4. Let's take a walk on a __________ day.
   맑은 날에 산책 하자.

5. It is too __________ today. 오늘 너무 덥다.

D He is great!

보기 same wonderful important kind

1. Sihu is very __________. 시후는 아주 친절하다.

2. We play soccer together on the __________ team.
   우리는 같은 팀에서 축구를 함께 해.

3. He gets many __________ goals!
   그는 많은 멋진 골들을 넣어!

4. He is an __________ member of this team.
   그는 이 팀의 중요한 멤버야.

정답과 해설 p.5

Practice 2 형용사를 써서 문장을 완성해 보아요.

다음 우리말 뜻과 같도록 주어진 표현을 순서에 맞게 배열하여 문장을 완성하세요.

1. (full, I, am).
나 배불러.

➔ I am full.

2. (I, angry, am)!
나 화났어!

➔ ______________________!

3. (famous, You, are). 당신은 유명합니다.
➔ ______________________.

4. (nice, can't say, anything, You). 너는 어떤 멋진 것도 말할 수 없다.
➔ ______________________.

5. (a, different, want, result, I). 나는 다른 결과를 원한다.
➔ ______________________.

6. (You, honest, are). 너는 정직해.
➔ ______________________.

7. (Sunday, is, favorite day, my). 일요일은 내가 가장 좋아하는 날이야.
➔ ______________________.

8. (is, big, ugly, and, He). 그는 (덩치가) 크고 못생겼어.
➔ ______________________.

정답과 해설 p.5

9. (He, strange, looks). 그는 이상해 보여.

➔ ____.

10. *Mother* : Please don't talk to strangers!

엄마 : 제발 낯선 사람들과 말하지 마라!

Red Riding Hood : Don't worry, mommy!

(I, be, careful, will)

빨간 모자 : 걱정하지 마세요, 엄마! 제가 조심할게요.

➔ Don't worry, mommy! ______________________________.

11. (your hands, Why, are, dirty)? 왜 당신의 손은 지저분해요?

➔ ____?

12. (am, sleepy, I). 나는 졸려.

➔ ______________________________________.

13. (not, crazy, I, am). 나는 미치지 않았어.

➔ ____.

14. (am, I, short). 나는 키가 작아.

➔ ______________________________________.

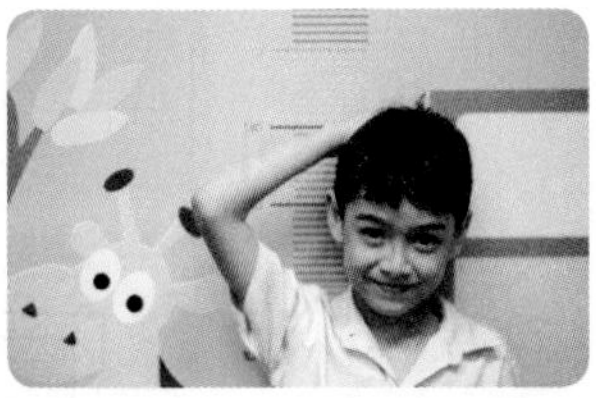

15. (don't have, any special, I, talents). 나는 어떠한 특별한 재능도 가지고 있지 않다.

➔ ____.

16. (is, He, brave). 그는 용감하다.

➔ ____.

정답과 해설 p.5

17. (alone, I, am).

나는 혼자야.

➔ ______________________.

18 . (is, This, diary, my new).

이건 나의 새 일기장이야.

➔ ______________________.

19. (a bad, choice, is, That) 그건 나쁜 선택이구나.

➔ ____.

20. (news, We have, good) for you. 우리는 너를 위한 좋은 소식을 갖고 있어.

➔ ______________________________ for you.

Cultural Tips

재미로 익히는 문화상식

나이 세기

James

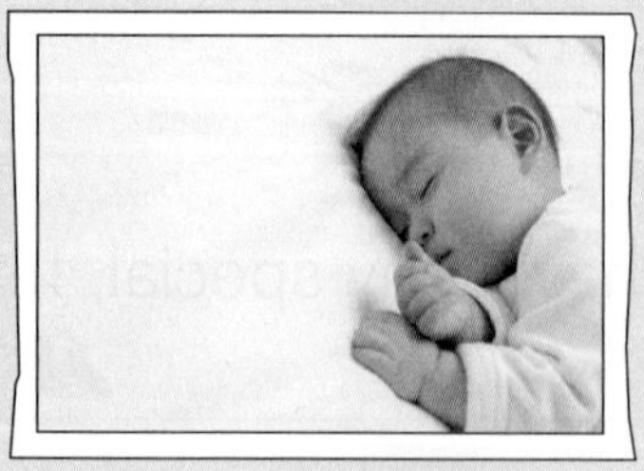

Minho

James와 민호는 2016년 3월 31일에 태어났어요. 그렇다면 2023년 3월 31일에 James와 민호는 각각 몇 살일까요? 둘 다 8살 아니냐구요? 민호는 8살이지만, James는 7살이랍니다!
한국에서는 아기가 엄마의 뱃속에 있을 때부터 나이를 세지만, 미국에서는 태어난 날부터 나이를 세기 때문이에요.
똑같은 날에 태어났는데 나이가 다르다니, 신기하죠?

정답과 해설 p.5

Practice 3 형용사를 써서 문장을 완성해 보아요.

우리말 뜻을 참고하여 다음 주어진 표현을 사용해 문장을 완성해 보세요. (필요시 어형을 바꿀 것)

1. (My dog, friendly)
나의 개는 사람을 잘 따라.

➔ My dog is friendly.

2. (mean)
그는 짓궂어.

➔ ______________________.

3. (Today, a hard day) 오늘은 힘든 날이야.
➔ ______________________.

4. (The English test, difficult) 영어 시험은 어려워.
➔ ______________________.

5. (be tired) 나 지쳤어.
➔ ______________________.

6. (That, nice, advice) 그것 참 멋진 충고구나.
➔ ______________________.

7. (The dog, have, short, legs) 그 개는 짧은 다리들을 갖고 있어(다리가 짧아).
➔ ______________________.

8. (This milk, be, fresh) 이 우유는 신선해.
➔ ______________________.

9. (The tortoise, slow) 그 거북이는 느리다.
➔ ______________________.

정답과 해설 p.5

10. (The cat, cute)

그 고양이는 귀여워.

➔ ______________________________.

11. (The park, beautiful)

그 공원은 아름다워.

➔ ______________________________.

12. (hungry) 나 배고파.

➔ ____.

13. (kind) 그녀는 그녀의 애완동물들에게 친절해.

➔ ____ to her pets.

14. (Dogs, loyal) 개들은 충직하다.

➔ ____.

15. (The car, expensive)

그 차는 비싸다.

➔ ______________________________.

16. (want, a yummy cake)

나는 맛있는 케이크를 원해.

➔ ______________________________.

17. (We, ready) 우리는 준비가 됐어.

➔ ____.

정답과 해설 p.6

18. (Jane, a good voice) Jane은 좋은 목소리를 갖고 있다.

➔ ____.

19. (The baby, lovely)

그 아기는 사랑스러워.

➔ ____________________

____________________.

20. (a long letter)

그는 그의 어머니께 긴 편지를 쓴다.

➔ ____________________

to his mother.

Cultural Tips 재미로 익히는 문화상식

다른 나라의 낮잠 풍습 - 시에스타(Siesta)

네, 맞아요. 다른 나라에는 시에스타라는 낮잠 시간이 있답니다.
이탈리아 · 그리스 등의 지중해 연안 국가와 라틴 아메리카의 낮잠 풍습을 말하는 것인데, 한낮의 무더위를 피해 활기를 회복하기 위한 전통이에요.
이탈리아에서는 오후 1시부터 3시 30분까지, 스페인에서는 오후 1시부터 4시까지, 그리스에서는 오후 2시부터 4시까지로 시간은 나라마다 차이가 있어요!
시에스타 중에는 일반 상점들뿐만 아니라 관공서도 문을 닫고 낮잠을 즐겨요.

정답과 해설 p.6

Let's Practice More!

SET 01

학습목표 1 | 여러 가지 형용사를 알아보아요. 공부한 날 : 맞은 개수 : /12개

밑줄 친 단어가 형용사면 ○표, 아니면 ×표를 하세요.

01. The park is beautiful. → ○
그 공원은 아름답다.

02. He runs fast. 그는 빨리 달려. → ______

03. A cheetah is very fast. 치타는 매우 빨라. → ______

04. An ant is tiny. 개미는 작아. → ______

05. A snail moves slowly. → ______
달팽이는 느리게 움직여.

06. A tortoise is slow. → ______
거북이는 느려.

07. Today is a hard day. 오늘은 힘든 날이야. → ______

08. She studies hard. 그녀는 열심히 공부해. → ______

09. My dog is friendly. → ______
나의 개는 사람을 잘 따라.

10. It is rainy today. 오늘 비 와. → ______

11. It rains heavily. 비가 엄청나게 내린다. → ______

12. It is too humid. 너무 습하다. → ______

정답과 해설 p.6

Let's Practice More!

SET 02

학습목표 1 | 여러 가지 형용사를 알아보아요. 공부한 날 : 맞은 개수 : /14개

다음 ( ) 안에서 알맞은 것을 고르세요.

01. You have (white shoes / shoes white). 너는 하얀 신발을 가지고 있네.

02. A snail is (slowly / slow). 달팽이는 느리다.

03. He wears a (black coat / coat black). 그는 검은 코트를 입어.

04. We have (news bad / bad news) for you. 우리는 너에게 줄 나쁜 소식이 있어.

05. Janet is a (famous singer / singer famous). Janet은 유명한 가수야.

06. My puppy is (friendly / friend). 나의 강아지는 사람을 잘 따라.

07. I am (full / fully). 나 배불러.

08. Your hands are (dirt / dirty). 너의 손은 더러워.

09. The math test is (easily / easy). 그 수학 시험은 쉬워.

10. I don't like a (room dark / dark room). 나는 어두운 방을 좋아하지 않아.

11. You look (strange / strangely). 너 이상해 보인다.

12. That is a (good idea / idea good)! 그거 좋은 생각이야!

13. Today is a (day windy / windy day). 오늘은 바람 부는 날이야.

14. I am (short / shortly). 난 키가 작아.

정답과 해설 p.6

Let's Practice More!

SET 03

학습목표 1 | 여러 가지 형용사를 알아보아요.　　공부한 날 :　　맞은 개수 :　　/14개

다음 우리말 해석을 보고 주어진 철자로 시작하는 단어를 완성해 보세요.

01. Do you like s___weet___ candies? 너는 달콤한 사탕을 좋아해?

02. I like s__________ jelly candy like Trolli.
나는 트롤리 같은 신 젤리를 좋아해.

03. Lee Sumin is a f__________ entertainer for teenagers.
이수민은 10대들에게 유명한 연예인이야.

04. It is r__________ today. 오늘 비 와.

05. I don't like w__________ days. 나는 바람이 많이 부는 날을 좋아하지 않아.

06. Let's take a walk on a s__________ day. 맑은 날에 산책 하자.

07. It is too h__________ today. 오늘 너무 덥다.

08. I am t__________. 나는 키가 커.

09. The park is b__________. 그 공원은 아름다워.

10. The dog has s__________ legs. 그 개는 다리가 짧아.

11. I like w__________ hugs. 난 따뜻한 포옹을 좋아해.

12. I have a y__________ umbrella. 나는 노란 우산을 가지고 있어.

13. I'm t__________. 나는 목이 말라.

14. The cat is c__________. 그 고양이는 귀여워.

정답과 해설 p.6

Let's Practice More!

SET 04

학습목표 2 | 형용사의 역할에 대해 알아보아요. 공부한 날 : 맞은 개수 : /12개

다음 밑줄 친 단어가 명사를 꾸며주는 역할이면 '수식'을, 보어 역할이면 '보어'를 쓰세요.

01. I'm thirsty. → 보어
나는 목이 말라.

02. She is pretty. → ______
그녀는 예뻐.

03. I don't like windy days. → ______
나는 바람이 많이 부는 날을 좋아하지 않아.

04. I am angry! → ______
나는 화났어!

05. That is a bad choice. → ______
그것은 안 좋은 선택이야.

06. My dog is friendly. → ______
내 개는 사람을 잘 따라.

07. Today is a hard day. → ______
오늘은 힘든 하루야.

08. He looks strange. → ______
그는 이상해 보여.

09. I will be careful. → ______
나는 조심할 거야.

10. I want a different result. → ______
나는 다른 결과를 원해.

11. This pizza smells good. → ______
이 피자는 맛있는 냄새가 나.

12. Your cat is so cute. → ______
너의 고양이는 너무 귀여워.

정답과 해설 p.6

Let's Practice More!

SET 05

학습목표 2 | 형용사의 역할에 대해 알아보아요.   공부한 날 :   맞은 개수 :   /14개

다음 우리말과 같은 뜻이 되도록 괄호 안에서 알맞은 것을 고르세요.

01. You look (nice / nicely) in that skirt.
너 그 치마 입으니까 멋져 보여.

02. The park is (beauty / beautiful). 그 공원은 아름다워.

03. The English test is (difficult / difficulty). 그 영어 시험은 어려워.

04. The baby is (love / lovely). 그 아기는 사랑스러워.

05. He looks (strangely / strange). 그는 이상해 보여.

06. I don't like (wind / windy) days. 나는 바람이 많이 부는 날을 좋아하지 않아.

07. My dog is (smart / smartly). 나의 개는 영리해.

08. You are (honesty / honest). 너는 정직해.

09. I will be (careful / carefully). 제가 조심할게요.

10. I am (sleep / sleepy). 나는 졸려.

11. Sihu is very (kind / kindly). 시후는 아주 친절하다.

12. I am (full / fully). 난 배불러.

13. This pizza smells (good / well). 이 피자는 맛있는 냄새가 나.

14. He gets (wonder / wonderful) goals! 그는 멋진 골들을 넣어!

정답과 해설 p.6

Let's Practice More!

SET 06

학습목표 3 | 형용사의 특징에 대해 알아보아요. 공부한 날 : 맞은 개수 : /14개

다음 ( ) 안에서 올바른 것을 고르세요.

01. I need (hot something / something hot).
나는 뜨거운 무언가가 필요해.

02. I have an (early dinner / dinner early). 나는 이른 저녁을 먹어.

03. I don't have any (special talents / talents special).
나는 어떠한 특별한 재능도 가지고 있지 않아.

04. We have (good news / news good) for you. 우리는 너를 위한 좋은 소식을 가지고 있어.

05. That is a (choice bad / bad choice). 그건 나쁜 선택이야.

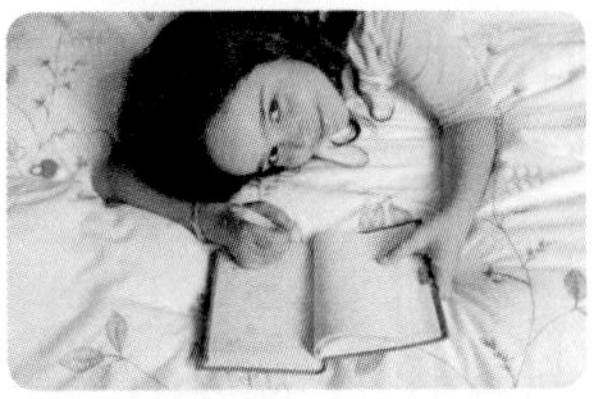

06. This is my (diary new / new diary).
이건 내 새로운 일기장이야.

07. I want (something sweet / sweet something). 나는 달콤한 무언가를 원해.

08. That is (nice advice / advice nice). 그것 참 멋진 충고구나.

09. The dog has (short legs / legs short). 그 개는 다리가 짧아.

10. There was (new nothing / nothing new) in his idea.
그의 제안에는 어떤 새로운 것도 없었어.

11. Do you like (sweet candies / candies sweet)? 너는 달콤한 사탕을 좋아하니?

12. He writes a (letter long / long letter). 그는 긴 편지를 써.

13. Jane has a (good voice / voice good).
Jane은 좋은 목소리를 가지고 있어.

14. I like (hugs warm / warm hugs).
나는 따뜻한 포옹을 좋아해.

정답과 해설 p.6

Let's Practice More!

SET 07

학습목표 4 | **형용사를 이용해 다양한 문장을 만들어 보아요.** 공부한 날 : 맞은 개수 : /20개

다음 우리말 해석에 맞게 주어진 문장에 ( ) 안의 단어를 넣어 문장을 완성해 보세요.

01. He gets goals! (wonderful)

→ He gets wonderful goals!

그는 멋진 골들을 넣어!

02. The dog has legs. (short)

→ ______________________.

그 개는 다리가 짧아.

03. You can say something. (nice)

→ ______________________. 너는 상냥한 무언가를 말할 수 있어.

04. Do you like candies? (sweet)

→ ______________________? 너는 달콤한 사탕을 좋아해?

05. I like hugs. (warm)

→ ______________________. 난 따뜻한 포옹을 좋아해.

06. Jane has a voice. (good)

→ ______________________. Jane은 좋은 목소리를 갖고 있다.

07. He writes a letter to his mother. (long)

→ ______________________. 그는 그의 어머니께 긴 편지를 쓴다.

08. That is advice. (nice)

→ ______________________. 그것 참 멋진 충고구나.

09. Today is a day. (hard)

→ ______________________. 오늘은 힘든 날이야.

정답과 해설 p.6

10. We have news for you. (good)

➔ ____.

우리는 너를 위한 좋은 소식을 갖고 있어.

11. I want a result. (different)

➔ ____.

나는 다른 결과를 원한다.

12. I don't like days. (windy)

➔ ____.

나는 바람이 많이 부는 날을 좋아하지 않아.

13. Let's take a walk on a day. (sunny)

➔ ____. 맑은 날에 산책 하자.

14. That is a choice. (bad)

➔ ____. 그건 나쁜 선택이구나.

15. This is my diary. (new)

➔ ____. 이건 나의 새 일기장이야.

16. Sunday is my day. (favorite)

➔ ____. 일요일은 내가 가장 좋아하는 날이야.

17. We play soccer together on the team. (same)

➔ ____.

우리는 같은 팀에서 축구를 함께 해.

18. He is a member of this team. (important)

➔ ____. 그는 이 팀의 중요한 멤버야.

19. I don't have any talents. (special)

➔ ____. 나는 어떠한 특별한 재능도 가지고 있지 않다.

20. I like jelly like Trolli. (sour)

➔ ____.

나는 트롤리 같은 신 젤리를 좋아해.

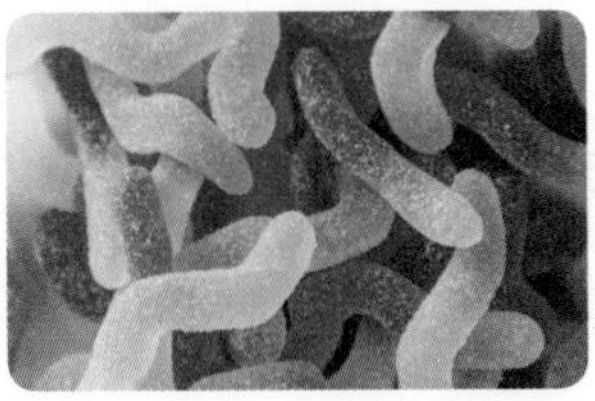

정답과 해설 p.6

Let's Practice More!

SET 08

학습목표 4 | **형용사를 이용해 다양한 문장을 만들어 보아요.** 공부한 날 : 맞은 개수 : /20개

다음 우리말 해석에 맞게 주어진 표현을 이용해서 문장을 완성해 보세요. (단, 필요한 경우 동사를 넣어 쓰세요.)

01. 이 우유는 신선해.
(This milk, fresh)

➜ This milk is fresh.

02. 너의 손은 지저분해.
(Your hands, dirty)

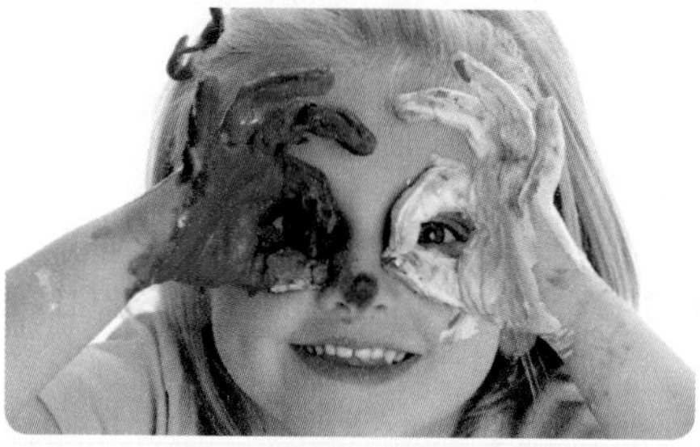

➜ ______________________.

03. 너의 고양이는 귀여워. (cat, cute)

➜ ______________________.

04. Janet은 예쁜 소녀야. (Janet, a pretty girl)

➜ ______________________.

05. 그것 참 멋진 충고구나. (That, nice advice)

➜ ______________________.

06. 너무 습하다. (too, humid)

➜ ______________________.

07. 그 영어시험은 어려워. (The English test, difficult)

➜ ______________________.

08. 그 개는 다리가 짧아. (The dog, short, legs)

➜ ______________________.

09. 시후는 친절하다. (Sihu, kind)

➜ ______________________.

정답과 해설 p.6

10. 너의 햄스터는 귀여워. (Your hamster, cute)

➔ ______________________________.

11. 난 배불러. (full)

➔ ______________________________.

12. 그녀는 그녀의 애완동물들에게 친절해. (kind, to her pets)

➔ ______________________________.

13. 그 아기는 사랑스러워. (The baby, lovely)

➔ ______________________________.

14. 오늘은 힘든 날이야. (Today, a hard day)

➔ ______________________________.

15. Jane은 좋은 목소리를 갖고 있다. (Jane, a good voice)

➔ ______________________________.

16. 이 피자는 맛있는 냄새가 나. (This pizza, smell, good)

➔ ______________________________.

17. 우리는 좋은 소식을 갖고 있어. (have, good, news)

➔ ______________________________.

18. 그는 멋진 골들을 넣어! (get, wonderful, goals)

➔ ______________________________!

19. 그는 중요한 멤버야. (an important member)

➔ ______________________________.

20. 개들은 충직하다. (Dogs, loyal)

➔ ______________________________.

정답과 해설 p.7

Chapter 03 부사

이 챕터에서는 행동이나 일의 상태, 특징을
설명하는 말인 '부사'에 대해 배워 보아요.

☆ 학습 방향 및 배울 내용 미리보기 ☆

Unit 01 : I'm very hungry.
부사의 기능과 모양
부사의 기능과 모양에 대해서 알아보아요.

▼

Unit 02 : I am usually free on Sundays.
주의해야 할 부사 / 빈도부사
주의해야 할 부사와 일이 벌어지는 횟수(빈도)를 나타내는 빈도부사에 대해 알아보아요.

단어 미리보기

이 챕터에 나올 단어들 중 이미 알고 있는 단어가 있나요?
맞는 뜻을 골라 체크해 봐요.

날짜 : 이름 : 알고 있는 단어의 수 : /24개

No.	아는 단어	단어	품사	알맞은 뜻에 체크 표시해 봐요.			
1	☑	sadly	부사	슬프게	☑	화나서	☐
2	☐	newly	부사	최근에	☐	새롭게	☐
3	☐	simply	부사	간단하게	☐	어렵게	☐
4	☐	friendly	형용사	친근한	☐	나쁜	☐
5	☐	quickly	부사	느리게	☐	빠르게	☐
6	☐	lovely	형용사	사랑스러운	☐	사랑의	☐
7	☐	always	부사	가끔	☐	항상	☐
8	☐	loudly	부사	시끄럽게	☐	작게	☐
9	☐	well	부사	좋게	☐	부드럽게	☐
10	☐	usually	부사	자주	☐	보통	☐
11	☐	free	형용사	한가한	☐	바쁜	☐
12	☐	wrong	형용사	옳은	☐	잘못된	☐
13	☐	borrow	동사	빌리다	☐	빌려주다	☐
14	☐	watch	명사	시간	☐	시계	☐
15	☐	lose	동사	잃어버리다	☐	찾다	☐
16	☐	never	부사	가끔	☐	전혀~하지 않는	☐
17	☐	cry	동사	웃다	☐	울다	☐
18	☐	still	부사	아직도	☐	함께	☐
19	☐	right	형용사	옳은	☐	잘못된	☐
20	☐	finish	동사	끝내다	☐	시작하다	☐
21	☐	leaf	명사	꽃	☐	잎	☐
22	☐	strongly	부사	강하게	☐	약하게	☐
23	☐	dangerous	형용사	위험한	☐	조심스러운	☐
24	☐	perfectly	부사	완벽하게	☐	서투르게	☐

UNIT 01 **부사의 기능과 모양**

I'm very hungry.

❖ POiNT 1 ❖

부사는 '천천히, 매우'처럼 행동이나 일의 상태, 특징을 설명하는 말이에요.

부사는 동사, 형용사, 다른 부사 그리고 문장 전체를 꾸며줘요.

동사 수식	My grandfather talks **slowly**. 나의 할아버지는 천천히 말씀하신다.
형용사 수식	I'm **very** hungry. 난 매우 배고파.
다른 부사 수식	She can run **very** fast. 그녀는 아주 빨리 달릴 수 있다.
문장 전체 수식	**Honestly**, I can't believe it. 솔직히, 저는 그것을 믿을 수 없어요.

❖ POiNT 2 ❖

부사의 모양

대부분의 형용사 형용사+ -ly	slow(느린)+-ly → slowly(느리게) safe(안전한)+-ly → safely(안전하게) sad(슬픈)+-ly → sadly(슬프게) new(새로운)+-ly → newly(새롭게)
자음+y로 끝나는 형용사 -y를 i로 바꾸고+ -ly	busy(바쁜)+-ly → busily(바쁘게) angry(화난)+-ly → angrily(화나서) happy(행복한)+-ly → happily(행복하게)
-le로 끝나는 형용사 -le를 빼고+ -ly	simple(간단한)+-ly → simply(간단하게) terrible(끔찍한)+-ly → terribly(끔찍하게)

＊참고

명사+-ly는 부사가 아닌 형용사예요!

friend(친구)+-ly → friendly(친근한)
love(사랑)+-ly → lovely(사랑스러운)

Check and Write

다음 문장에서 부사를 찾아 동그라미 해보세요.

1. I walk slowly.

나는 느리게 걸어.

2. My father works busily.

우리 아빠는 바쁘게 일하셔.

3. Sihu quickly raises his hand.

시후는 재빨리 그의 손을 들어올린다.

4. Junwoo played the drum loudly.

준우는 시끄럽게 드럼을 쳤어.

5. I touched it softly.

나는 그것을 부드럽게 만졌어.

정답과 해설 p.7

UNIT

02 I am usually free on Sundays.

주의해야 할 부사 / 빈도부사

❖ POiNT 1 ❖

주의해야 할 부사

형용사와 모양이 같은 부사	fast(빠른) – fast(빨리)
	early(이른) – early(일찍)
	late(늦은) – late(늦게)
	high(높은) – high(높게)
	hard(열심인) – hard(열심히)
형용사와 모양이 완전히 다른 부사	good(좋은) – well(좋게, 잘)

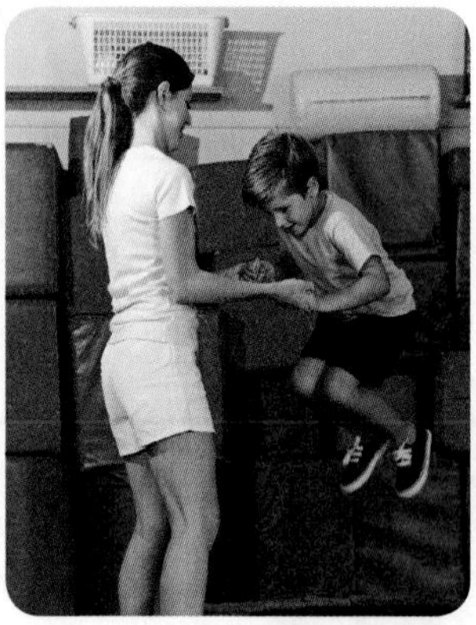

❖ POiNT 2 ❖

빈도부사는 일이 벌어지는 횟수(빈도)를 나타내는 부사예요.

빈도부사는 조동사와 be동사 뒤에, 일반동사 앞에 쓰여요.

100%	always (항상)
90%	usually (보통)
70%	often (자주)
50%	sometimes (가끔)
10%	seldom (거의 ~하지 않는)
0%	never (전혀 ~하지 않는)

I will **always** love you. 난 항상 널 사랑할 거야.

I am **usually** free on Sundays. 난 보통 일요일에 한가해.

Jihye **often** buys books. 지혜는 자주 책을 사.

We **sometimes** do the wrong things.
우리는 가끔 잘못된 일을 해.

He **seldom** reads the newspaper.
그는 신문을 거의 읽지 않아.

Heungbu : Can I borrow some rice?
흥부 : 쌀 조금만 빌릴 수 있을까요?
Nolbu's wife : We have no rice! 우린 쌀이 없어!
놀부의 아내 **Never** come back! 절대 돌아오지 마!

[흥부와 놀부]

Check and Write

A **다음 밑줄 친 단어가 형용사인지 부사인지 구분해보세요.**

1. She runs fast. 그녀는 빨리 달려. [부사]
2. My watch is fast. 내 시계는 빨라. [ ]
3. I'm late. 나는 늦었어. [ ]
4. I get up late. 나는 늦게 일어나. [ ]
5. Sihu is a good friend. 시후는 좋은 친구야. [ ]
6. He plays soccer well. 그는 축구를 잘해. [ ]

B **다음 ( ) 안에서 올바른 것을 고르세요.**

1. I (often lose / lose often) my smartphone.
   나는 자주 내 스마트폰을 잃어버려.

2. I (always am / am always) happy.
   나는 항상 행복해.

3. I (can never / never can) tell a lie.
   나는 절대 거짓말할 수 없어.

정답과 해설 p.7

Practice 1 상황에 맞는 적절한 부사를 익혀 보아요.

주어진 우리말 뜻을 참고하여 보기에서 알맞은 부사를 골라 써 보세요.

A So many animals!

보기 again well slowly often high so

1. I ___often___ go to the zoo. 나는 동물원에 자주 가.

2. Monkeys climb trees __________.
원숭이들은 나무를 잘 타.
3. The lion walks __________. 사자는 느리게 걸어.
4. The kangaroo jumps __________. 캥거루는 높이 뛰어.
5. The panda eats __________ many bamboo leaves.
팬더는 매우 많은 대나무 잎을 먹어.
6. I want to visit the zoo __________. 나는 동물원을 다시 방문하고 싶어.

B Dance festival

보기 together hard happily quickly loudly

1. Bora wants to join the dance festival. 보라는 댄스 페스티벌에 참가하기를 원해.
She practices __________ with Junwoo. 그녀는 준우와 열심히 연습해.
2. Bora and Junwoo dance __________. 보라와 준우는 함께 춤을 춰.
3. Junwoo learns to dance __________. 준우는 춤추는 것을 빨리 배워.
4. She plays the music __________.
그녀는 음악을 크게 틀어.
5. They dance __________. 그들은 행복하게 춤을 춰.

정답과 해설 p.7

C Lucy is very busy!

보기 later fast quickly always exactly so hard late

1. Lucy gets up __________ in the morning.
   Lucy는 아침에 늦게 일어나.

2. She runs __________ to school.
   그녀는 학교로 빨리 뛰어가.

3. She doesn't have to run __________ fast.
   그녀는 그렇게 빨리 달리지 않아도 돼.

4. Lucy studies __________. Lucy는 열심히 공부해.

5. She must finish her homework __________.
   그녀는 그녀의 숙제를 빨리 끝내야만 해.

6. She wants to play with her dog __________.
   그녀는 나중에 그녀의 개와 놀기를 원해.

7. She says, "I __________ feel safe with my dog."
   그녀는 말한다, "난 항상 나의 개와 함께 있으면 안심이 돼."

8. That's __________ right. 그것은 정확히 맞아.

정답과 해설 p.7

Practice 2 문장에 쓰인 부사를 확인해 보아요.

다음 우리말 해석의 밑줄 친 부분에 해당하는 부사를 주어진 문장에서 찾아 빈칸에 써 보세요.

1. It snows heavily.
눈이 펑펑 내린다.

→ heavily

2. She cooks well.
그녀는 요리를 잘해.

→

3. The children run fast to the playground.
아이들이 운동장으로 빨리 뛰어간다. →

4. They play hard. 그들은 열심히 놀아. →

5. They smile happily. 그들은 행복하게 웃어. →

6. Hayul cries loudly. 하율이는 시끄럽게 울어. →

7. He is too young. 그는 너무 어려. →

8. Life doesn't always go easily.
인생은 항상 쉽게 흘러가지는 않는다. →

정답과 해설 p.7

9. He looks very nice.

그는 매우 멋져 보여.

10. They work hard. 그들은 열심히 일한다.

11. We are still on summer vacation. 우리는 아직 여름방학 중이다.

12. We have dinner slowly.

우리는 천천히 저녁을 먹어.

13. I am very fond of sunsets. (*be fond of: ~을 좋아하다, sunset: 해질녘, 일몰)

나는 해질녘을 매우 좋아해.

14. Where is he? I can't even see him.

그는 어디 있어? 나는 그를 볼 수조차 없어.

15. Honestly, I can't believe it.

솔직히, 나는 그것을 믿을 수 없어요.

16. She always goes to school with her little brother.

그녀는 항상 그녀의 남동생과 함께 학교에 간다.

정답과 해설 p.7

17. We play soccer together. 우리는 함께 축구를 한다. ➔

18. He cleans his room perfectly. ➔

그는 그의 방을 완벽하게 청소한다.

19. They usually go to the movies on Saturdays. ➔

그들은 보통 토요일에 영화를 보러 간다.

20. You must move quickly.

너는 빨리 움직여야 해. ➔

Cultural Tips

재미로 익히는 문화상식

시간에 따라 다른 인사법을 가진 나라들

morning
아침

Good morning! (굿모닝)

おはよう! (오하요오)

안녕!

day
낮

Good afternoon! (굿 애프터눈)

こんにちは! (곤니찌와)

안녕!

evening
저녁

Good evening! (굿 이브닝)

こんばんは! (곰방와)

안녕!

우리나라는 언제 만나든지 인사가 똑같지만, 다른 나라에서는 시간에 따라 인사법이 달라요!
잘 기억해 두면 좋겠죠?

정답과 해설 p.7

Practice 3 부사의 적절한 쓰임을 익혀 보아요.

다음 ( )안에서 알맞은 것을 고르고 문장을 다시 써 보세요.

1. I sleep (deeply / deep).
나는 잠을 깊이 잔다.

➔ I sleep deeply.

2. She walks (fast / fastly).
그녀는 빨리 걷는다.

➔ ________________.

3. It is (already / alreadily) 11:00 p.m. 벌써 밤 11시야.

➔ ________________________________.

4. When can we (meet again / again meet)? 우리 언제 또 만날 수 있지?

➔ ________________________________?

5. Junwoo wakes up (lately / late). 준우는 늦게 일어난다.

➔ ________________________________.

6. Our English teacher (very is / is very) kind.
우리 영어 선생님은 매우 친절하셔.

➔ ________________.

7. It's (dangerous too / too dangerous). (*dangerous: 위험한)
그것은 너무 위험하다.

➔ ________________.

정답과 해설 p.7

8. He can (today go to school / go to school today). 그는 오늘 학교에 갈 수 있어.

➔ ____.

9. He goes to school (early / earlily). 그는 학교에 일찍 가.

➔ ____.

10. Mom (says often / often says) that. 엄마는 그것을 자주 말해요.

➔ ____.

11. I (really / real) like movies. 난 정말 영화를 좋아해.

➔ ____.

12. He (still is / is still) in the hospital.
그는 아직도 병원에 있다.

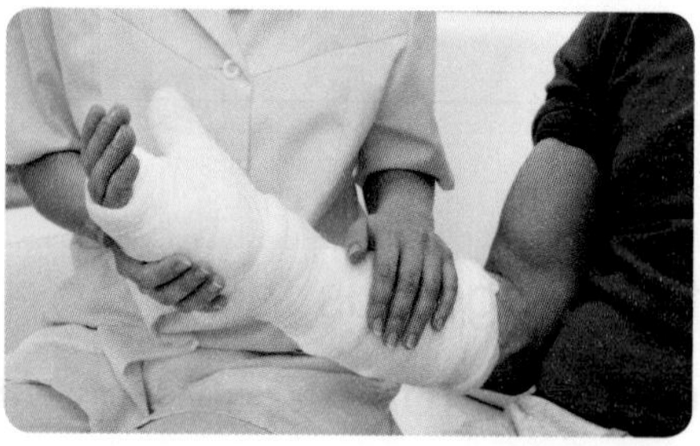

➔ ______________________

______________________.

13. We cross (safe / safely) at the crosswalk.
우리는 안전하게 횡단보도를 건넌다.

➔ ______________________

______________________.

14. He (has never / never has) breakfast. 그는 아침을 전혀 먹지 않는다.

➔ ____.

정답과 해설 p.7

15. My aunt drives (carefully / careful). 나의 이모는 조심히 운전하셔.

➔ ____.

16. Mina (takes always / always takes) piano lessons.
미나는 항상 피아노 수업을 들어.

➔ ____.

17. She (seldom / hard) eats chocolate.
그녀는 초콜릿을 거의 먹지 않아.

➔ ____________________.

18. He ties them (strongly / strong). (*tie: 묶다, 매다)
그는 그것들을 단단하게 묶어요.

➔ ____________________.

19. She speaks (angry / angrily). 그녀는 화나서 말해.

➔ ____.

20. You can (loudly speak / speak loudly). 너는 크게 말할 수 있어.

➔ ____.

정답과 해설 p.7

Let's Practice More!

SET 01

학습목표 1 | **여러 가지 부사를 익혀 보아요.** 공부한 날 : 맞은 개수 : /12개

다음 형용사에 -ly를 붙여 부사로 바꿔 보세요.

01. slow 느린 ➔ slowly 느리게

02. happy 행복한 ➔ ______ 행복하게

03. safe 안전한 ➔ ______ 안전하게

04. new 새로운 ➔ ______ 새롭게

05. sad 슬픈 ➔ ______ 슬프게

06. quick 빠른 ➔ ______ 빠르게

07. simple 간단한 ➔ ______ 간단하게

08. busy 바쁜 ➔ ______ 바쁘게

09. angry 화난 ➔ ______ 화나서

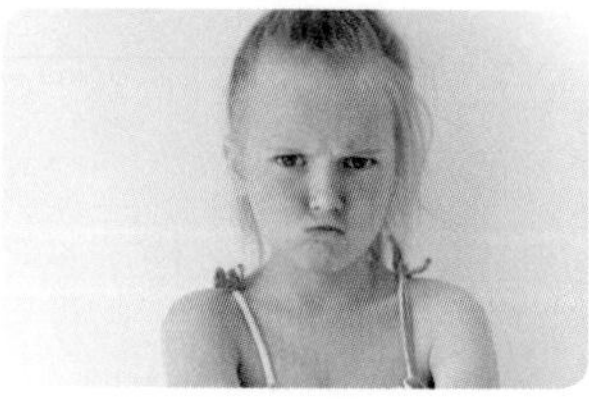

10. loud 시끄러운 ➔ ______ 시끄럽게

11. terrible 끔찍한 ➔ ______ 끔찍하게

12. soft 부드러운 ➔ ______ 부드럽게

정답과 해설 p.8

Let's Practice More!

SET 02

학습목표 1 | 여러 가지 부사를 익혀 보아요. 공부한 날 : 맞은 개수 : /14개

다음 밑줄 친 부사가 맞으면 ○표, 틀리면 고쳐 쓰세요.

01. I solved the problem simplely. 나는 그 문제를 간단히 풀었어. → simply

02. The lion walks slowly. 사자는 느리게 걸어. → ______

03. My aunt drives carefuly. 나의 이모는 조심히 운전하셔. → ______

04. She plays the music loudly. 그녀는 음악을 크게 틀어. → ______

05. We cross safly at the crosswalk. 우리는 안전하게 횡단보도를 건넌다. → ______

06. She must finish her homework quickly. 그녀는 숙제를 빨리 끝내야만 해. → ______

07. It snows heavvyly. 눈이 펑펑 내린다. → ______

08. Honestly, I can't believe it. 솔직히, 나는 그것을 믿을 수 없어요. → ______

09. He cleans his room perfectly. 그는 그의 방을 완벽하게 청소한다. → ______

10. They smile gentlely. 그들은 상냥하게 웃어. → ______

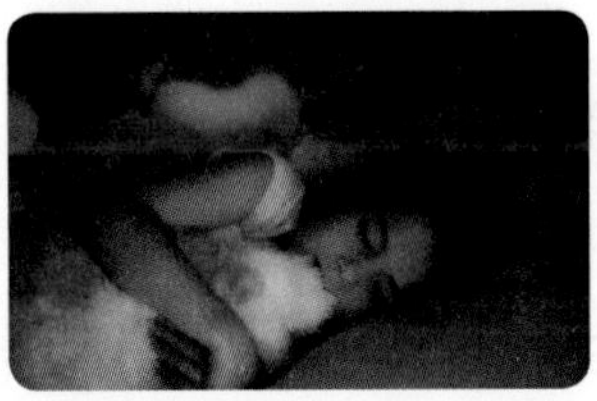

11. I sleep deeply. 나는 잠을 깊이 잔다. → ______

12. Life doesn't always go easyly. 인생은 항상 쉽게 흘러가지는 않는다. → ______

13. He ties them strongly. 그는 그것들을 단단하게 묶어요. → ______

14. She shouts angryly. 그녀는 화나서 소리쳐. → ______

정답과 해설 p.8

Let's Practice More!

SET 03

학습목표 1 | 여러 가지 부사를 익혀 보아요.   공부한 날 :   맞은 개수 :   /14개

다음 문장에서 부사를 찾아 ○표 하세요.

01. Bora dances happily. 보라는 행복하게 춤춰.

02. Monkeys climb trees well. 원숭이들은 나무를 잘 타.

03. The kangaroo jumps high. 캥거루는 높이 뛰어.

04. Bora and I dance together. 보라와 나는 함께 춤을 춰.

05. She practices hard with Mike. 그녀는 Mike와 열심히 연습해.

06. Junwoo learns to dance quickly. 준우는 춤추는 것을 빨리 배워.

07. Lucy gets up late in the morning. Lucy는 아침에 늦게 일어나.

08. She runs fast to school. 그녀는 학교로 빨리 뛰어가.

09. That's exactly right. 그것은 정확히 맞아.

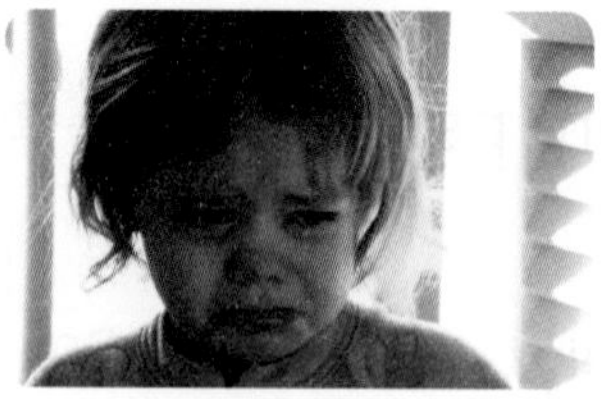

10. Hayul cries loudly. 하율이는 시끄럽게 울어.

11. I really like movies. 난 정말 영화를 좋아해.

12. I want to visit the zoo again. 나는 동물원을 다시 방문하고 싶어.

13. They smile happily. 그들은 행복하게 웃어.

14. She wants to play with her dog later.
그녀는 나중에 그녀의 개와 놀기를 원해.

정답과 해설 p.8

Let's Practice More!

SET 04

학습목표 2 | 부사의 쓰임을 익혀 보아요. 공부한 날 : 맞은 개수 : /12개

밑줄 친 단어가 형용사를 수식하면 '형', 동사를 수식하면 '동', 부사를 수식하면 '부'를 쓰세요.

01. I'm <u>very</u> hungry. 나는 매우 배고파. → 형

02. She walks <u>very</u> slowly. 그녀는 아주 느리게 걷는다. → ______

03. Junwoo wakes up <u>late</u>. 준우는 늦게 일어난다. → ______

04. Our English teacher is <u>very</u> kind. 우리 영어 선생님은 매우 친절하셔. → ______

05. We cross <u>safely</u> at the crosswalk. 우리는 안전하게 횡단보도를 건넌다. → ______

06. He is <u>too</u> young. 그는 너무 어려. → ______

07. He goes to school <u>early</u>. 그는 학교에 일찍 가. → ______

08. She doesn't have to run <u>so</u> fast. 그녀는 그렇게 빨리 달리지 않아도 돼. → ______

09. That's <u>exactly</u> right. 그것은 정확히 맞아. → ______

10. I <u>really</u> like movies. 난 정말 영화를 좋아해. → ______

11. He looks <u>very</u> nice. 그는 매우 멋져 보여. → ______

12. I sleep <u>deeply</u>. 나는 잠을 깊이 잔다. → ______

정답과 해설 p.8

Let's Practice More!

SET 05

학습목표 3 | 형용사와 부사를 구분해 보아요. 공부한 날 : 맞은 개수 : /14개

밑줄 친 단어가 형용사면 '형', 부사면 '부'를 쓰세요.

01. Honestly, I can't believe it. 솔직히, 나는 그것을 믿을 수 없어. → 부

02. I have a friendly friend. 나는 다정한 친구가 있어. → ______

03. He goes to school early. 그는 학교에 일찍 가. → ______

04. We have an early dinner. 우리는 이른 저녁을 먹어. → ______

05. This ring has a high price. 이 반지는 가격이 비싸. → ______

06. The kangaroo jumps high. 캥거루는 높이 뛰어. → ______

07. She is a lovely girl. 그녀는 사랑스러운 소녀야. → ______

08. Lucy gets up late in the morning. Lucy는 아침에 늦게 일어나. → ______

09. Don't be late. 늦지 마. → ______

10. She speaks angrily. 그녀는 화나서 말해. → ______

11. They run fast to school. 그들은 학교로 빨리 뛰어가. → ______

12. This book is hard to understand. 이 책은 이해하기 어려워. → ______

13. Lucy studies hard. Lucy는 열심히 공부해. → ______

14. He cooks well. 그는 요리를 잘해. → ______

정답과 해설 p.8

Let's Practice More!

SET 06

학습목표 4 | 문장에서 빈도부사의 올바른 위치에 대해 알아보아요. 공부한 날 : 맞은 개수 : /14개

다음 밑줄 친 부사의 위치가 맞으면 ○표, 틀리면 ×표를 하세요.

01. She loses often her wallet. 그녀는 자주 그녀의 지갑을 잃어버려. → ×

02. I always feel safe with my dog. 난 항상 나의 개와 함께 있으면 안심이 돼. → ______

03. I usually am free on Saturdays. 나는 보통 토요일에 한가해. → ______

04. He takes always piano lessons. 그는 항상 피아노 수업을 들어. → ______

05. I often go to the zoo. 나는 동물원에 자주 가. → ______

06. I will always support you. 난 항상 널 응원할 거야. → ______

07. She seldom eats chocolate. 그녀는 초콜릿을 거의 먹지 않아. → ______

08. Mom says often that. 엄마는 그것을 자주 말해요. → ______

09. I sometimes can help your work. 나는 가끔 너의 일을 도와줄 수 있어. → ______

10. He never has breakfast. 그는 아침을 전혀 먹지 않는다. → ______

11. They play usually badminton on Sundays. 그들은 보통 일요일에 배드민턴을 친다. → ______

12. She is always kind. 그녀는 항상 친절해. → ______

13. He never will tell the truth. 그는 절대 진실을 말하지 않을 거야. → ______

14. She always goes to school with her brother. 그녀는 항상 그녀의 오빠와 함께 학교에 간다. → ______

정답과 해설 p.8

Let's Practice More!

SET 07

학습목표 4 | 문장에서 빈도부사의 올바른 위치에 대해 알아보아요. 공부한 날 : 맞은 개수 : /20개

다음 ( ) 안에서 올바른 것을 고르세요.

01. I will (always love / love always) you. 나는 항상 너를 사랑할 거야.

02. She (eats seldom / seldom eats) broccoli.
그녀는 브로콜리를 거의 먹지 않아.

03. He (has never / never has) breakfast. 그는 아침을 전혀 먹지 않는다.

04. I (usually am / am usually) busy on Mondays. 나는 보통 월요일에 바쁘다.

05. Mom (often nags / nags often) me. (*nag: 잔소리를 하다)
엄마는 자주 나에게 잔소리를 해요.

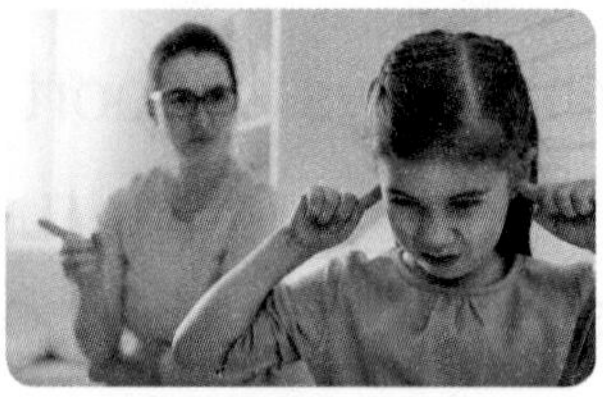

06. They (usually go / go usually) to the movies on Saturdays.
그들은 보통 토요일에 영화를 보러 간다.

07. Hayul (cries often / often cries) loudly. 하율이는 종종 시끄럽게 울어.

08. You (are always / always are) right. 네가 항상 맞아.

09. Lucy (never studies / studies never) hard.
Lucy는 전혀 공부를 열심히 하지 않아.

10. I (usually arrive / arrive usually) at school on time.
나는 보통 학교에 제시간에 도착해.

정답과 해설 p.8

11. I (never can / can never) tell my secret. 나는 절대 내 비밀을 말할 수 없다.

12. We (usually play / play usually) soccer together after school.
우리는 보통 방과 후에 함께 축구를 한다.

13. He (cleans often / often cleans) his room. 그는 자주 그의 방을 청소한다.

14. My grandfather (usually talks / talks usually) slowly.
나의 할아버지는 보통 천천히 말하신다.

15. You can (always speak / speak always) confidently. (*confidently: 자신 있게)
넌 항상 자신있게 말할 수 있어.

16. They (always work / work always) hard.
그들은 항상 열심히 일한다.

17. I (go often / often go) to the museum. 나는 박물관에 자주 가.

18. She (is always / always is) positive. (*positive: 긍정적인)
그녀는 항상 긍정적이야.

19. They (seldom lose / lose seldom) the game. 그들은 경기에서 거의 지지 않는다.

20. They (go usually / usually go) shopping on Fridays.
그들은 보통 금요일에 쇼핑을 간다.

정답과 해설 p.8

Let's Practice More!

SET 08

학습목표 5 | 부사의 모양과 쓰임을 확실히 다져 보아요. 공부한 날 : 맞은 개수 : /20개

다음 ( ) 안의 단어 중 맞는 것에 ○표 하세요.

01. He jumps (high / highly).
그는 높이 뛰어.

02. Jake (simplely / simply) loves to sing.
Jake는 그저 노래 부르는 것을 좋아해.

03. Life doesn't always go (easy / easily).
인생은 항상 쉽게 흘러가지는 않아.

04. She practices (hard / hardly) with Junwoo.
그녀는 준우와 함께 열심히 연습해.

05. It snows (heavy / heavily).
눈이 펑펑 내려.

06. Lucy gets up (late / lately) in the morning.
Lucy는 아침에 늦게 일어나.

07. I want to visit the zoo (again / againly).
나는 동물원을 다시 방문하고 싶어.

08. She wants to play with her dog (lately / later).
그녀는 나중에 그녀의 개와 함께 놀기를 원해.

09. She runs (fast / fastly) to school.
그녀는 학교로 빨리 뛰어가.

10. She cooks (well / good).
그녀는 요리를 잘해.

정답과 해설 p.8

11. We cross (safe / safely) at the crosswalk.
우리는 안전하게 횡단보도를 건너.

12. That skirt suits her (good / well). (*suit: 어울리다)
저 치마는 그녀에게 잘 어울린다.

13. My aunt drives (careful / carefully).
나의 이모는 조심히 운전하셔.

14. He goes to school (early / earlily).
그는 일찍 학교로 가.

15. (Honesty / Honestly), I can't believe it.
솔직히, 나는 그것을 믿을 수 없어.

16. I (real / really) like my friends.
나는 나의 친구들을 정말 좋아해.

17. It is (already / alreadily) 11:00 p.m.
벌써 밤 11시야.

18. You have to use a knife (carefully / careful).
너는 칼을 조심히 사용해야 해.

19. You must move (quick / quickly).
너는 빨리 움직여야 해.

20. He (often / oftenly) goes to the music concert.
그는 음악 콘서트에 자주 가.

정답과 해설 p.8

실전테스트 CHAPTER 01~03

공부한 날 :
복습한 날 :
부모님 확인 :

CHAPTER 01 조동사 CHAPTER 02 형용사 CHAPTER 03 부사

●정답과 해설은 별책 8쪽에서 확인하세요!!

01

다음 조동사와 일반동사가 바른 순서로 된 것을 고르세요.

(1) You (must go, go must) there.
(2) I (go can, can go) anywhere.

[02~05] 다음 밑줄 친 부분을 바르게 고쳐 문장을 다시 쓰세요.

02

You must <u>does</u> your homework.

⇨ ______________________________

03

She can <u>cooks</u> this soup.

⇨ ______________________________

04

He has to <u>speaks</u> English.

⇨ ______________________________

05

You may <u>had</u> a seat.

⇨ ______________________________

[06~10] 다음 우리말 해석과 같도록 빈칸에 알맞은 빈도부사를 쓰세요.

06

He s__________ smiles.
(그는 거의 웃지 않는다.)

07

I a__________ smile.
(나는 항상 웃는다.)

08

She n__________ smiles.
(그녀는 절대 웃지 않는다.)

09

You s__________ smile.
(너는 가끔 웃는다.)

10

They o__________ smile.
(그들은 종종 웃는다.)

[11~13] 다음 그림을 보고, 우리말 뜻과 같도록 빈칸에 알맞은 조동사를 쓰세요.

11

You __________ __________ wash your hands before lunch.
(너는 점심식사 전에 손을 씻어야 해.)

12

He __________ play the guitar.
(그는 기타를 칠 수 있어.)

13

I __________ write a letter to Dan.
(나는 Dan에게 편지를 써야 해.)

14

다음 문장을 부정문으로 바르게 고친 것을 고르세요.

He has to fix the computer.

① He doesn't has to fix the computer.
② He doesn't have to fix the computer.
③ He has not to fix the computer.
④ He don't have to fix the computer.

15

다음 문장의 밑줄 친 Can과 쓰임이 같은 문장을 고르세요.

<u>Can</u> I borrow your pen?

① I <u>can</u> understand you.
② You <u>can</u> take a rest.
③ He <u>can</u> remember many things.
④ She <u>can</u> swim well.

16

다음 밑줄 친 부분을 바르게 고치세요.

It smells <u>strangely</u>.

→ __________

실전테스트

[17~18] 그림을 보고, 우리말 뜻과 같도록 빈칸에 알맞은 형용사를 쓰세요.

17

She is ___________.

(그녀는 아름답다.)

18

She is ___________.

(그녀는 키가 크다.)

19

다음 그림을 보고, 빈칸에 들어갈 알맞은 단어를 고르세요.

A: Do you know her?
B: Yes, I do. She is our English teacher. She is very _________.

① kind ② angrily
③ happily ④ carefully

[20~22] 다음 중 형용사를 고르세요.

20

① clearly ② quickly
③ strong ④ nicely

21

① glad ② slowly
③ greatly ④ happily

22

① friendly ② quietly
③ busily ④ strangely

23

다음 표의 빈칸에 [보기]의 단어를 알맞게 분류해서 쓰세요.

[보기] always kind rainy honestly happily

형용사	부사

[24~25] 다음 중 형용사를 부사로 잘못 바꾼 것을 고르세요.

24

① careful – carefully
② quick – quickly
③ easy – easyly
④ wide – widely

25

① late – late
② hard – hard
③ nice – nicly
④ cold – coldly

26

우리말 해석과 같도록 빈칸에 들어갈 알맞은 말을 고르세요.

그녀는 항상 버스를 타고 학교에 간다.
= She ________ goes to school by bus.

① sometimes ② always
③ usually ④ never

[27~30] 다음은 민호의 일주일 일과표입니다. 표를 보고 빈칸에 알맞은 말을 [보기]에서 골라 쓰세요.

	월	화	수	목	금	토	일
Have breakfast with his family	V	V	V	V	V	V	V
Read books							
Play baseball		V					
Help his mother	V				V	V	V

[보기] always, sometimes, never, seldom

27

He ________ helps his mother.

28

He ________ reads books.

29

He ________ has breakfast with his family.

30

He ________ plays baseball.

Chapter 04 감탄문

이 챕터에서는 기쁨, 놀람, 슬픔의 감정을 나타낼 때 쓰는
문장인 '감탄문'에 대해 배워 보아요.

☆ 학습 방향 및 배울 내용 미리보기 ☆

☐ Unit 01 : What a kind girl she is!

What으로 시작하는 감탄문

감탄하는 부분이 명사일 때 사용하는 What으로 시작하는 감탄문에 대해 알아보아요.

▼

☐ Unit 02 : How tall he is!

How로 시작하는 감탄문

감탄하는 부분에 형용사나 부사가 포함되어 있을 때 사용하는 How로 시작하는 감탄문에 대해 알아보아요.

단어 미리보기

이 챕터에 나올 단어들 중 이미 알고 있는 단어가 있나요?
맞는 뜻을 골라 체크해 봐요.

날짜 : 　　　　이름 : 　　　　알고 있는 단어의 수 : 　　　　/24개

No.	아는 단어	단어	품사	알맞은 뜻에 체크 표시해 봐요.			
1	☑	kind	형용사	친절한	☑	사랑스러운	☐
2	☐	interesting	형용사	재미없는	☐	재미있는	☐
3	☐	easy	형용사	어려운	☐	쉬운	☐
4	☐	make	동사	만들다	☐	요리하다	☐
5	☐	exciting	형용사	흥미로운	☐	썰렁한	☐
6	☐	spring	명사	가을	☐	봄	☐
7	☐	hot	형용사	차가운	☐	뜨거운	☐
8	☐	weather	명사	일기	☐	날씨	☐
9	☐	swim	동사	뛰다	☐	수영하다	☐
10	☐	smile	동사	웃다	☐	울다	☐
11	☐	nice	형용사	못된	☐	친절한	☐
12	☐	active	형용사	활동적인	☐	소극적인	☐
13	☐	surprise	명사	뜻밖의 일	☐	선물	☐
14	☐	library	명사	도서관	☐	음악실	☐
15	☐	large	형용사	작은	☐	큰	☐
16	☐	excellent	형용사	훌륭한	☐	별 볼일 없는	☐
17	☐	lazy	형용사	부지런한	☐	게으른	☐
18	☐	puppy	명사	강아지	☐	고양이	☐
19	☐	feet	명사	팔	☐	발	☐
20	☐	dark	형용사	밝은	☐	어두운	☐
21	☐	train	명사	기차	☐	비행기	☐
22	☐	fur	명사	수염	☐	털	☐
23	☐	peaceful	형용사	평온한	☐	시끄러운	☐
24	☐	draw	동사	돌다	☐	그림을 그리다	☐

UNIT

01 What a kind girl she is!

What으로 시작하는 감탄문

❖ POiNT 1 ❖

감탄문은 기쁨, 놀람, 슬픔의 감정을 나타낼 때 쓰는 문장으로 What이나 How로 시작하고 끝에 느낌표를 붙여요!

What	What a kind girl she is! 그녀는 매우 친절한 소녀구나!
How	How fast he runs! 그는 매우 빨리 달리는구나!

❖ POiNT 2 ❖

What으로 시작하는 감탄문은 '매우 ~한 (명사)구나!'라는 뜻이에요.
감탄하는 부분이 명사일 때 사용해요!

평서문 : 주어 + 동사 + a very + 형용사 + 명사.
감탄문 : What + (a/an) + 형용사 + 명사 + (주어 + 동사)!

※ 뒤의 **주어 + 동사**는 생략하는 경우가 많아요!

※ What 뒤에 셀 수 있는 단수명사가 올 때 부정관사 a/an을 써줘요!

It is | a very beautiful flower.
그것은 매우 아름다운 꽃이다.

What a beautiful flower | (it is)!
매우 아름다운 꽃이구나!

※ 감탄하는 부분이 복수명사일 경우 what + 형용사 + 복수명사 + (주어 + 동사)!로 쓸 수 있어요.
⇨ What beautiful stars! 정말 아름다운 별들이구나!

Check and Write

A 다음 빈칸에 들어갈 말로 알맞은 것을 보기에서 골라 써 보세요.

보기	very	What	a	an

1. She makes a [very] delicious cake.
그녀는 매우 맛있는 케이크를 만들어.

2. [ ] a delicious cake she makes!
그녀가 만드는 케이크가 참 맛있구나!

3. It is [ ] very easy game.
그것은 매우 쉬운 게임이야.

4. What [ ] easy game it is!
그것은 아주 쉬운 게임이구나!

B 다음 문장을 감탄문으로 고쳐 보세요.

1. This is a very funny dog.
이것은 아주 웃긴 강아지야.
→ What a funny dog (this is)!
(이것은) 아주 웃긴 강아지구나!

2. This is a very exciting game.
이건 아주 흥미로운 놀이야.
→ ______________________!
(이건) 아주 흥미로운 놀이구나!

정답과 해설 p.9

UNIT

02 How tall he is!

How로 시작하는 감탄문

❖ POiNT ❖

How로 시작하는 감탄문은 '~이 매우 (형용사/부사)하구나!'라는 뜻이에요!
감탄하는 부분에 명사 없이 형용사나 부사만 포함되어 있을 때 사용해요.

평서문 : 주어 + 동사 + very + 형용사(부사).
감탄문 : How + 형용사(부사) + (주어 + 동사)!

※ 감탄문 끝에 오는 주어와 동사는 생략할 수 있어요!

The flower is | very beautiful.

그 꽃은 매우 아름다워.

How beautiful | the flower is!

매우 아름다운 꽃이구나!

She studies | very hard.

그녀는 아주 열심히 공부해.

How hard | she studies!

그녀는 아주 열심히 공부하는구나!

He is | very tall.

그는 아주 키가 커.

How tall | he is!

그는 아주 키가 크구나!

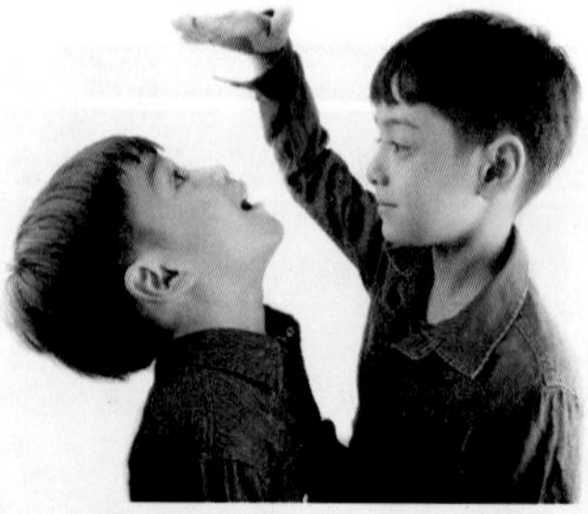

Check and Write

A 다음 빈칸에 들어갈 말로 알맞은 것을 보기에서 골라 써 보세요.

보기	is	How	high	very

1. He is [very] cute.
   그는 아주 귀여워.

2. [ ] cute he [ ]!
   그는 아주 귀엽구나!

3. They jump [ ] high.
   그들은 아주 높이 뛰어.

4. How [ ] they jump!
   그들은 아주 높이 뛰는구나!

B 다음 문장을 감탄문으로 고쳐 보세요.

1. She is very smart.
   그녀는 매우 똑똑해.
   ➔ How smart she is!
   그녀는 매우 똑똑하구나!

2. He looks very happy.
   그는 아주 행복해 보여.
   ➔ ______________________!
   그는 아주 행복해 보이는구나!

정답과 해설 p.9

Practice 1 상황에 맞는 적절한 감탄문을 익혀 보아요.

주어진 우리말 뜻을 참고하여 보기 에서 알맞은 말을 골라 빈칸에 써 보세요.

A A beautiful day

보기 How what beautiful spring

1. It is a <u>beautiful</u> day. 아름다운 날이다.
2. Yes, ________ a beautiful day it is! 맞아, 매우 아름다운 날이구나!
3. ________ warm it is! 정말 따뜻하구나!
4. What a wonderful ________! 아주 멋진 봄이구나!

B A beautiful beach

보기 beautiful cold ice cream What How well

1. It is a ________ beach. 아름다운 해변이다.
2. ________ beautiful it is! 그것은 정말 아름답구나!
3. ________ hot weather it is! 날씨가 참 덥구나!

4. How ________ she swims!
   그녀는 수영을 정말 잘하는구나!
5. What delicious ________ it is!
   그것은 매우 맛있는 아이스크림이구나!
6. How ________ it is! 그거 정말 차갑다!

정답과 해설 p.9

C My friend

보기 What kind friend very How

1. __________ broadly she smiles! (*broadly: 활짝)
그녀는 참 활짝 웃는구나!

2. She is __________ smart. 그녀는 매우 똑똑해요.

3. __________ a smart elementary school student!
아주 똑똑한 초등학생이구나!

4. How __________ she is! 그녀는 아주 친절하구나!

5. What a good __________! 참 좋은 친구다!

D At school

보기 very What nice How question

1. What a difficult __________! 정말 어려운 문제구나!

2. I don't understand. __________ difficult!
이해가 안 된다. 매우 어렵구나!

3. __________ a smart teacher! 참 똑똑하신 선생님이구나!

4. She's __________ kind. She always answers with a smile.
그녀는 매우 친절해요. 그녀는 항상 웃으면서 대답해 주세요.

5. How __________ she is! 그녀는 아주 친절하구나!

정답과 해설 p.9

Practice 2 What, How를 써서 감탄문을 완성해 보아요.

다음 우리말 뜻과 같도록 주어진 표현을 순서에 맞게 배열하여 문장을 완성하세요.

1. (an, active girl, What)!
아주 활동적인 소녀구나! (*active: **활동적인, 활발한**)

➔ What an active girl !

2. (delicious, How, it is)!
그것은 정말 맛있구나!

➔ ____________________ !

3. (good idea, a, What)! 아주 좋은 생각이구나!
➔ ____________________ !

4. (tall tree, What, a)! 매우 큰 나무구나!
➔ ____________________ !

5. (funny, How)! 정말 재미있구나!
➔ ____________________ !

6. (How, answers, slowly, she)! 그녀는 정말 천천히 대답하는구나!
➔ ____________________ !

7. (fast, runs, How, he)! 그는 참 빠르게 달리는구나!
➔ ____________________ !

8. (a, wonderful day, What)! 아주 멋진 날이구나!
➔ ____________________ !

9. (How, the dinner, smells, great)! 저녁 식사 냄새가 참 좋구나!
➔ ____________________ !

10. (waste of time, a, What)! (*waste: **낭비**) 완전히 시간 낭비야!
➔ ____________________ !

정답과 해설 p.9

11. (an, honor, What)!
아주 영광스럽구나!

➔ ______________________________!

12. (your mom, How, cooks, well)! 너희 엄마는 요리를 참 잘하시는구나!

➔ ______________________________!

13. (clean, How)! 정말 깨끗하구나!

➔ ______________________________!

14. (a, What, happy day)! 정말 행복한 하루구나!

➔ ______________________________!

15. (What, pleasant surprise, a)! (*surprise: 뜻밖의 일, 놀라움)
정말 뜻밖의 기분 좋은 일이구나!

➔ ______________________________!

16. (lovely voice, a, What)! 정말 사랑스러운 목소리구나!

➔ ______________________________!

17. (How, the dog, is, lazy)! 그 개는 정말 게으르구나!

➔ ______________________________!

18. (What, lovely cat, a)! 정말 사랑스러운 고양이구나!

➔ ______________________________!

19. (pity, a, What)! (*pity: 애석한 일, 동정) 참 애석한 일이구나!

➔ ______________________________!

20. (well, How, she, plays) hide-and-seek! (*hide-and-seek: 숨바꼭질)
그녀는 숨바꼭질을 참 잘하는구나!

➔ ______________________________ hide-and-seek!

정답과 해설 p.9

Practice 3 What, How를 써서 감탄문을 완성해 보아요.

우리말 뜻을 참고하여 주어진 표현을 사용해 문장을 완성해 보세요.
(단, 주어가 3인칭 단수일 때에는 동사를 알맞게 변형하세요.)

1. (an interesting book)

(그것은) 정말 흥미로운 책이구나!

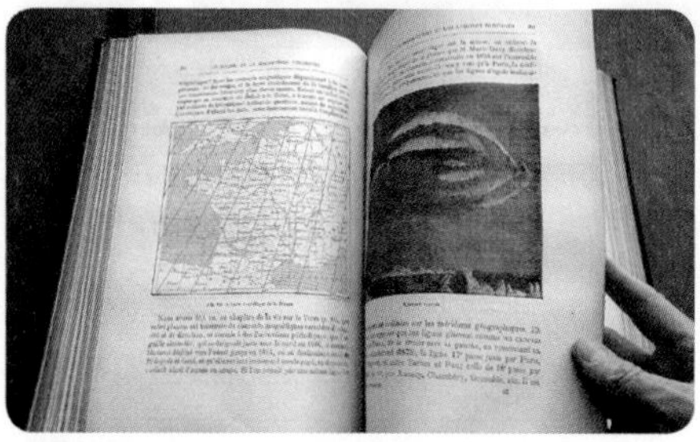

➔ What an interesting book (it is)!

2. (well, play the guitar)

그는 기타를 참 잘 연주하는구나!

➔ ______________________________!

3. (beautifully, sing) 그녀는 정말 아름답게 노래하는구나!

➔ ______________________________!

4. (a nice cover) (그것은) 아주 멋진 표지구나!

➔ ______________________________!

5. (an excellent picture) (그것은) 정말 훌륭한 그림이구나!

➔ ______________________________!

6. (a large library)

(그것은) 정말 큰 도서관이구나!

➔ ______________________________!

7. (big) (그것은) 아주 크구나!

➔ ______________________________!

정답과 해설 p.9

8. (a kind brother) (그는) 정말 친절한 오빠구나!

➔ ____!

9. (a heavy rain)

비가 정말 많이 오는구나!

➔ ____________________!

10. (loudly, bark) (*bark: (개가) 짖다)

그들은 매우 큰 소리로 짖는구나!

➔ ____________________!

11. (gently, speak) 그는 정말 온화하게 말을 하는구나!

➔ ____!

12. (a wonderful sister) (그녀는) 정말 멋진 누나구나!

➔ ____!

13. (well, draw) (*draw: 그림을 그리다)

너는 참 그림을 잘 그리는구나!

➔ ______________________________!

14. (tall) (그는) 정말 키가 크구나!

➔ ____!

15. (a cute puppy) (그것은) 정말 귀여운 강아지구나!

➔ ____!

16. (white, its fur) 그것의 털이 정말 하얗구나!

➔ ______________________________!

정답과 해설 p.9

17. (peaceful) (*peaceful: 평온한, 평화로운)

(그는) 정말 평온하구나!

➔ ______________________________!

18. (a fast train)

(그것은) 정말 빠른 기차구나!

➔ ______________________________!

19. (dark) 정말 어둡구나!

➔ ____!

20. (small, his feet) 그의 발은 정말 작구나!

➔ ____!

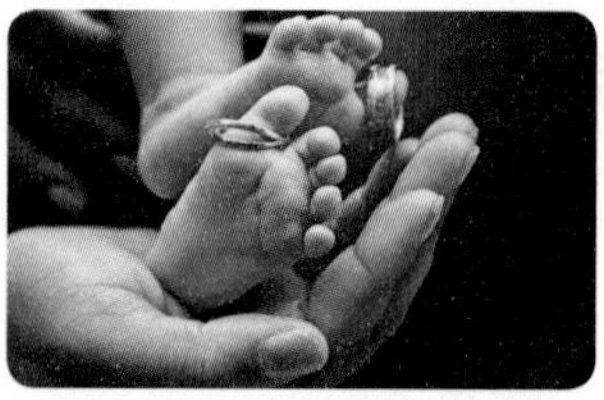

Cultural Tips 재미로 익히는 문화상식

여러 나라의 다양한 인사

정답과 해설 p.9

Let's Practice More!

SET 01

학습목표 1 | What과 How를 이용한 감탄문의 개념을 확실히 익혀 보아요. 공부한 날 : 맞은 개수 : /12개

What이나 How가 강조하는 표현이 명사면 '명', 형용사면 '형', 부사면 '부'라고 쓰세요.

01. How smart she is! → 형
그녀는 정말 똑똑해!

02. What a beautiful day it is! → ______
매우 아름다운 날이구나!

03. How nice she is! → ______
그녀는 아주 친절하구나!

04. What a smart teacher! → ______
참 똑똑하신 선생님이구나!

05. How warm it is! → ______
정말 따뜻하구나!

06. What a wonderful spring! → ______
아주 멋진 봄이구나!

07. How slowly she answers! → ______
그녀는 정말 천천히 대답하는구나!

08. What hot weather it is! → ______
날씨가 참 덥구나!

09. How well she swims! → ______
그녀는 수영을 매우 잘하는구나!

10. What delicious ice cream it is! → ______
그것은 매우 맛있는 아이스크림이구나!

11. How cold it is! → ______
그거 정말 차갑다!

12. How broadly she smiles! → ______
그녀는 참 활짝 웃는구나!

정답과 해설 p.9

Let's Practice More!

SET 02

학습목표 1 | What과 How를 이용한 감탄문의 개념을 확실히 익혀 보아요. 공부한 날 : 맞은 개수 : /14개

다음 빈칸에 What이나 How 중 알맞은 것을 골라 써보세요.

01. What a beautiful flower! 매우 아름다운 꽃이구나!

02. ________ kind she is! 그녀는 아주 친절하구나!

03. ________ a difficult question! 정말 어려운 문제구나!

04. ________ a cute puppy it is! 그것은 정말 귀여운 강아지구나!

05. ________ white its fur is! 그것의 털이 정말 하얗구나!

06. ________ peaceful he is! 그는 정말 평온하구나!

07. ________ an interesting book! 정말 흥미로운 책이구나!

08. ________ well he plays the guitar! 그는 기타를 참 잘 연주하는구나!

09. ________ beautifully she sings! 그녀는 정말 아름답게 노래하는구나!

10. ________ a fast train it is! 그것은 정말 빠른 기차구나!

11. ________ dark it is! 정말 어둡구나!

12. ________ small his feet are! 그의 발은 정말 작구나!

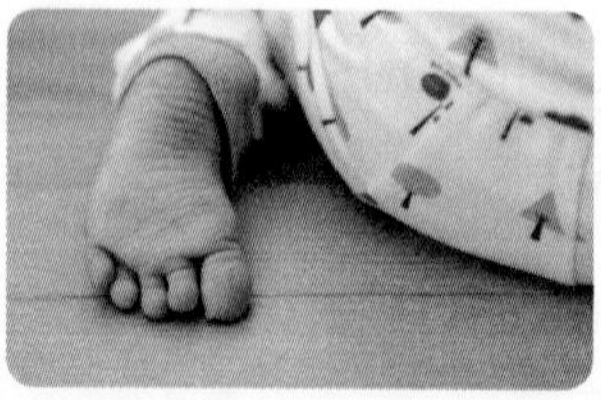

13. ________ a wonderful sister she is! 그녀는 정말 멋진 누나구나!

14. ________ gently he speaks! 그는 정말 온화하게 말을 하는구나!

정답과 해설 p.10

Let's Practice More!

SET 03

학습목표 1 | What과 How를 이용한 감탄문의 개념을 확실히 익혀 보아요. 공부한 날 : 맞은 개수 : /14개

다음 빈칸에 a나 an 중 알맞은 것을 골라 써보세요.

01. What ___a___ large library! 정말 큰 도서관이구나!

02. What ________ kind brother he is! 그는 정말 친절한 오빠구나!

03. What ________ active girl! 아주 활동적인 소녀구나!

04. What ________ smart elementary school student! 아주 똑똑한 초등학생이구나!

05. What ________ good friend! 참 좋은 친구구나!

06. What ________ interesting book it is! 그것은 정말 흥미로운 책이구나!

07. What ________ happy day! 행복한 하루구나!

08. What ________ excellent picture it is! 그것은 정말 훌륭한 그림이구나!

09. What ________ honor! 아주 영광스럽구나!

10. What ________ old house! 정말 낡은 집이구나!

11. What ________ pleasant surprise! 정말 뜻밖의 기분 좋은 일이구나!

12. What ________ amazing day! 정말 놀라운 날이구나!

13. What ________ lovely voice! 정말 사랑스러운 목소리구나!

14. What ________ tall tree! 매우 큰 나무구나!

정답과 해설 p.10

Let's Practice More!

SET 04

학습목표 2 | 감탄문의 순서를 익혀 보아요.

공부한 날 :　　　맞은 개수 :　　　/12개

다음 ( ) 안에서 알맞은 것을 고르세요.

01. (How fast / Fast how) he runs!
그는 매우 빨리 달리는구나!

02. (How great / Great how) the dinner smells! 저녁 식사 냄새가 참 좋구나!

03. (Clean how / How clean) the room is! 방이 정말 깨끗하구나!

04. (A happy day what / What a happy day) it is! 행복한 하루구나!

05. (Lazy how / How lazy) the dog is! 그 개는 정말 게으르구나!

06. (How well / Well how) she plays hide-and-seek! 그녀는 숨바꼭질을 참 잘하는구나!

07. (What a good idea / A good idea what) it is! 그것은 아주 좋은 생각이구나!

08. (Delicious how / How delicious) it is! 그것은 정말 맛있구나!

09. What a tall tree (it is / is it)! 그것은 매우 큰 나무구나!

10. How funny (are you / you are)! 너는 정말 재미있구나!

11. What a wonderful sister (she is / is she)! 그녀는 정말 멋진 누나구나!

12. How small (are his feet / his feet are)! 그의 발은 정말 작구나!

정답과 해설 p.10

Let's Practice More!

SET 05

학습목표 2 | 감탄문의 순서를 익혀 보아요. 공부한 날 : 맞은 개수 : /14개

다음 우리말 뜻과 같도록 주어진 표현들을 순서대로 배열해 보세요.

01.

(big / it is / How)!

그것은 정말 크구나!

➔ How big it is !

02.

(they bark / How / loudly)!

그들은 정말 큰 소리로 짖는구나!

➔ ______________________!

03. (she is / What / a kind girl)! 그녀는 정말 친절한 소녀구나!

➔ ______________________!

04. (a large library / What / it is)! 그것은 정말 큰 도서관이구나!

➔ ______________________!

05. (he is / a kind brother / What)! 그는 정말 친절한 남동생이구나!

➔ ______________________!

06. (a / What / rain / heavy)! 비가 정말 많이 오는구나!

➔ ______________________!

07. (a pleasant surprise / it is / What)! 그거 정말 뜻밖의 기분 좋은 일이구나!

➔ ______________________!

정답과 해설 p.10

08. (well / How / he / plays the guitar)! 그는 기타를 참 잘 연주하는구나!

➔ ____!

09. (it is / a / lovely voice / What)!

그것은 정말 사랑스러운 목소리구나!

➔ ____!

10. (your mom / well / How / cooks)!

너의 엄마는 요리를 정말 잘하시는구나!

➔ ______________________________________!

11. (What / an / it is / interesting book)! 그것은 정말 흥미로운 책이구나!

➔ ____!

12. (she / beautifully / How / sings)!

그녀는 정말 아름답게 노래하는구나!

➔ ______________________________________!

13. (What / it is / a nice cover)! 그것은 정말 멋진 표지구나!

➔ ____!

14. (it is / an / What / excellent picture)! 그것은 정말 훌륭한 그림이구나!

➔ ____!

정답과 해설 p.10

Let's Practice More!

SET 06

학습목표 2 | 감탄문의 순서를 익혀 보아요. 공부한 날 : 맞은 개수 : /14개

다음 감탄문의 순서가 맞으면 ○표, 틀리면 고쳐 써 보세요.

01. How he is tall! → How tall he is!
그는 키가 정말 크구나!

02. What it is a waste of time! → ____________
그것은 참 시간 낭비구나!

03. How dark it is! → ____________
아주 어둡구나!

04. How she smiles broadly! → ____________
그녀는 참 활짝 웃는구나!

05. What a cute puppy it is! → ____________
그것은 정말 귀여운 강아지구나!

06. How kind is she! → ____________
그녀는 정말 친절하구나!

07. What are you a good friend! → ____________
너는 정말 좋은 친구구나!

08. How white its fur is! → ____________
그것의 털은 정말 하얗구나!

09. What is it a difficult question! → ____________
그건 정말 어려운 질문이구나!

10. How she is nice! → ____________
그녀는 정말 친절하구나!

11. How peaceful he is! → ____________
그는 정말 평온하구나!

12. What it is a fast train! → ____________
그것은 정말 빠른 기차구나!

13. How his feet small are! → ____________
그의 발은 정말 작구나!

14. How difficult it is! → ____________
그것은 정말 어렵구나!

정답과 해설 p.10

Let's Practice More!

SET 07

학습목표 3 | 평서문을 감탄문으로 바꿔 보아요. 공부한 날 : 맞은 개수 : /20개

다음 평서문을 감탄문으로 바꿔 보세요. (단, 뒤의 주어와 동사까지 모두 쓰세요.)

01. 

This is a very funny story.

➜ What a funny story this is !

이건 정말 재미있는 책이구나!

02. 

It is very delicious ice cream.

➜ ______ !

그것은 정말 맛있는 아이스크림이구나!

03. It is a very beautiful day.

➜ ______ ! 정말 아름다운 날이구나!

04. She is very smart.

➜ ______ ! 그녀는 아주 똑똑하구나!

05. It is very hot weather.

➜ ______ !

날씨가 정말 덥구나!

06. She swims very well.

➜ ______ ! 그녀는 정말 수영을 잘하는구나!

07. It is very cold.

➜ ______ ! 그거 정말 차갑구나!

08. She answers very slowly.

➜ ______ ! 그녀는 정말 느리게 대답하는구나!

09. It is a very wonderful day.

➜ ______ ! 정말 멋진 날이구나!

정답과 해설 p.10

10. He runs very fast.

➜ ______________________________! 그는 아주 빨리 달리는구나!

11. It is a very lovely cat.

➜ ______________________________!

그것은 정말 사랑스러운 고양이구나!

12. Your mom cooks very well.

➜ ______________________________! 너의 어머니는 요리를 정말 잘하시는구나!

13. She is very beautiful.

➜ ______________________________! 그녀는 매우 아름답구나!

14. He is very kind.

➜ ______________________________! 그는 아주 친절하구나!

15. It is a very wonderful spring.

➜ ______________________________! 아주 멋진 봄이구나!

16. The dinner smells very great.

➜ ______________________________! 저녁 식사 냄새가 아주 훌륭하구나!

17. The elephant is very big.

➜ ______________________________! 그 코끼리는 정말 크구나!

18. You are very lazy.

➜ ______________________________! 너는 아주 게으르구나!

19. It is a very good idea.

➜ ______________________________! 그것은 아주 좋은 생각이구나!

20. Its fur is very white.

➜ ______________________________!

그것의 털은 아주 하얗구나!

정답과 해설 p.10

Let's Practice More!

SET 08

학습목표 4 | 감탄문을 평서문으로 만들어 보아요.　　공부한 날 :　　맞은 개수 :　　/20개

다음 감탄문을 평서문으로 만들어 보세요.

01.

How well he plays the flute!

➔ He plays the flute very well.

그는 플루트를 아주 잘 연주해.

02.

How clean the room is!

➔ ______________________________.

그 방은 매우 깨끗해.

03. What an interesting book it is!

➔ ______________________________. 그것은 아주 흥미로운 책이야.

04. How beautifully she sings!

➔ ______________________________. 그녀는 매우 아름답게 노래해.

05. What a nice cover it is!

➔ ______________________________. 그것은 아주 멋진 표지야.

06. What a happy day it is!

➔ ______________________________. 매우 행복한 날이야.

07. How great the dinner smells!

➔ ______________________________. 저녁 식사는 아주 훌륭한 냄새가 나.

08. What a tall tree it is!

➔ ______________________________.

그것은 아주 큰 나무야.

09. How big it is!

➔ ______________________________. 그것은 아주 커.

정답과 해설 p.10

10. What a kind brother he is!

→ ______________________________. 그는 아주 친절한 형이야.

11. 

What a heavy rain it is!

→ ______________________.

그것은 엄청난 폭우야.

12. 

What a pleasant surprise it is!

→ ______________________.

그것은 정말 뜻밖의 기분 좋은 일이야.

13. How loudly they bark!

→ ______________________________. 그들은 매우 크게 짖어.

14. How lazy the dog is!

→ ______________________________. 그 개는 아주 게을러.

15. What an amazing day it is!

→ ______________________________. 아주 놀라운 날이야.

16. How gently he speaks!

→ ______________________________. 그는 매우 부드럽게 말해.

17. What an active girl she is!

→ ______________________________. 그녀는 아주 활발한 소녀야.

18. What a good idea it is!

→ ______________________________. 그것은 아주 좋은 생각이야.

19. 

How well you draw!

→ ______________________.

너는 그림을 아주 잘 그려.

20. 

How well she plays hide-and-seek!

→ ______________________.

그녀는 숨바꼭질을 아주 잘해.

정답과 해설 p.11

Chapter 05 명령문

이 챕터에서는 말하는 이가 듣는 이에게 무엇을 시키거나 어떤 행동을 하도록 요구할 때 쓰는 문장인 '명령문'에 대해 배워 보아요.

☆ 학습 방향 및 배울 내용 미리보기 ☆

☐ **Unit 01 : Be** quiet.

긍정 명령문

긍정 명령문의 모양과 의미에 대해 알아보아요.

▼

☐ **Unit 02 : Don't** be afraid!

부정 명령문

부정 명령문의 모양과 의미에 대해 알아보아요.

단어 미리보기

이 챕터에 나올 단어들 중 이미 알고 있는 단어가 있나요?
맞는 뜻을 골라 체크해 봐요.

날짜 : 이름 : 알고 있는 단어의 수 : /24개

No.	아는 단어	단어	품사	알맞은 뜻에 체크 표시해 봐요.			
1	☑	open	동사	닫다	☐	펴다	☑
2	☐	quiet	형용사	조용한	☐	시끄러운	☐
3	☐	stand	동사	앉다	☐	일어서다	☐
4	☐	cheer up	동사	기운을 내다	☐	시무룩해지다	☐
5	☐	afraid	형용사	두려워하는	☐	친숙한	☐
6	☐	bite	동사	짖다	☐	물다	☐
7	☐	solve	동사	풀다	☐	찾다	☐
8	☐	give up	동사	이기다	☐	포기하다	☐
9	☐	pot	명사	냄비	☐	프라이팬	☐
10	☐	picnic	명사	수업	☐	소풍	☐
11	☐	watch out	동사	조심하다	☐	밖을 보다	☐
12	☐	have	동사	먹다	☐	뱉다	☐
13	☐	volume	명사	음량	☐	공책	☐
14	☐	second	형용사	첫 번째의	☐	두 번째의	☐
15	☐	truth	명사	거짓	☐	진실	☐
16	☐	forget	동사	잊다	☐	기억하다	☐
17	☐	mistake	명사	실수	☐	사과	☐
18	☐	sugar	명사	설탕	☐	사탕	☐
19	☐	ask	동사	대답하다	☐	묻다	☐
20	☐	mix	동사	풀다	☐	섞다	☐
21	☐	circle	명사	원	☐	사각형	☐
22	☐	pick	동사	꽂다	☐	꺾다	☐
23	☐	after	전치사	전에	☐	후에	☐
24	☐	insect	명사	곤충	☐	새	☐

UNIT

01 Be quiet.

긍정 명령문

❖ POiNT 1 ❖

명령문은 '~해라/~하지 마라'라고 명령하는 문장이에요!

긍정 명령문 Wake up. 일어나.

부정 명령문 Don't wake up. 일어나지 마.

❖ POiNT 2 ❖

긍정 명령문의 모양

명령문은 듣는 대상이 You(너, 당신)이기 때문에 주어를 생략해요!
그래서 긍정 명령문은 동사원형으로 시작하고, 해석은 '~해라'라고 해요.

평서문 You open your textbooks.
여러분은 여러분의 교과서를 폅니다.

명령문 Open your textbooks.
여러분의 교과서를 펴세요.

평서문 You are quiet.
너는 조용하다.

명령문 Be quiet.
조용히 해.

※ 명령문을 쓰면서도 듣는 사람의 기분이 나쁘지 않게 하려면, 공손한 느낌이 들도록 please(부디, 제발)를 붙여주면 돼요. please는 명령문의 앞에 쓸 수도 있고, 뒤에 쓸 수도 있어요.

Please stand up.
일어나세요.

Stand up, please.
일어나세요.

※ 명령문에 please를 붙이지 않더라도 어떤 목소리로, 어떤 표정으로 말하는지에 따라 의미가 많이 달라진답니다.

Check and Write

다음 문장을 긍정 명령문으로 고쳐보세요.

1. You wake up.

너는 일어난다.

➔ Wake up.

일어나.

2. You are careful.

너는 조심한다.

➔ ______________________.

조심해.

3. You look at me.

너는 나를 본다.

➔ ______________________.

나를 봐.

4. You take my hand.

너는 나의 손을 잡는다.

➔ ______________________.

내 손을 잡아.

5. You cheer up.

너는 힘을 낸다.

➔ ______________________.

힘내.

정답과 해설 p.11

UNIT

02 Don't be afraid!

부정 명령문

❖ POiNT ❖

부정 명령문의 모양

긍정 명령문과 마찬가지로 평서문의 부정형에서 주어를 생략해줘요!
즉, 동사원형 앞에 Don't를 붙여 주고 해석은 '~하지 마라'라고 해요.

평서문 You aren't afraid.
너는 두려워하지 않아.

명령문 Don't be afraid.
두려워하지 마.

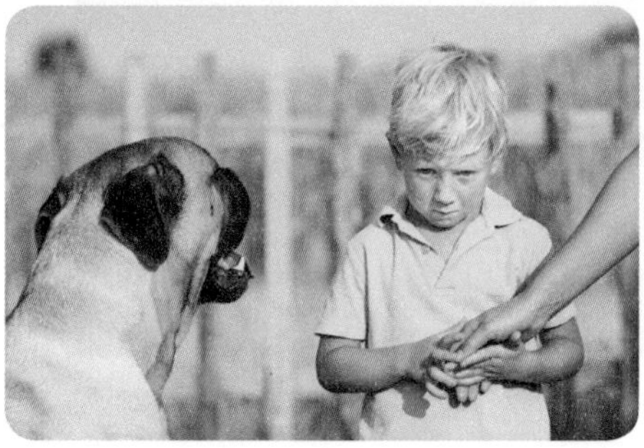

평서문 You don't do anything crazy.
너는 엉뚱한 짓을 하지 않아.

명령문 Don't do anything crazy.
엉뚱한 짓 하지 마.

평서문 You don't close the door.
너는 문을 닫지 않아.

명령문 Don't close the door.
문을 닫지 마.

Check and Write

다음 문장을 부정 명령문으로 고쳐보세요.

1. You don't bite.

너는 물지 않아.

➔ Don't bite.

물지 마.

2. You don't give up.

너는 포기하지 않아.

➔ ______________________.

포기하지 마.

3. You aren't late.

너는 늦지 않는다.

➔ ______________________.

늦지 마.

4. You don't fight with your brother.

너는 너의 남동생과 싸우지 않는다.

➔ ______________________.

너의 남동생과 싸우지 마.

5. You don't cry.

너는 울지 않는다.

➔ ______________________.

울지 마.

정답과 해설 p.11

Practice 1 명령문을 익혀 보아요.

주어진 우리말 뜻과 같도록 알맞은 표현을 보기 에서 골라 빈칸에 써 보세요.

A Before an exam

보기 Solve Wait Mark Don't speak Put

1. ___Put___ your books away. 여러분의 책들을 치우세요.

2. ________ the problems. 문제를 푸세요.

3. ________ your answers with a black pen.
답은 검정색 펜으로 표시하세요.

4. ________ until the time is up. (*until: ~까지)
시간이 다 끝날 때까지 기다리세요.

5. ________ during the exam. (*during: ~중에, ~동안에)
시험 중에는 얘기하지 마세요.

B Making ramen

보기 Put Boil Be Cook

1. ________ water. 물을 끓이세요.

2. ________ noodles and sauce into the pot.
면과 소스를 냄비에 넣으세요.

3. ________ for 5 minutes. 5분 동안 익히세요.

4. ________ careful because it is hot. 뜨거우니까 조심하세요.

정답과 해설 p.11

C School picnic

보기 Don't worry　watch out　Check　drive　get in

1. You are going on a picnic. __________ your bag.
너 소풍 가지. 가방을 확인해보렴.

2. __________, Mom. I have everything. 걱정하지 마세요, 엄마. 다 있어요.

3. Well, __________ for strangers. 음, 모르는 사람들 조심하고.

4. Okay, please __________ me to school. I am late. (*drive: ~을 태워다 주다)
네, 학교까지 태워다 주세요. 저 늦었어요.

5. Okay, __________ the car. 그래, 차에 타렴.

D It's a beetle!

보기 Look　Put　Don't bring　Come　Stop　Don't be

1. __________ here! 이리로 와봐!

2. What's the matter? __________ yelling.
무슨 일이야? 소리 좀 그만 질러.

3. __________ at this! It is a beetle! (*beetle: 딱정벌레)
이거 봐! 딱정벌레야!

4. __________ it away. I am afraid of insects. (*insect: 곤충)
저리 치워. 난 곤충이 무서워.

5. __________ afraid. It doesn't bite. 무서워하지 마. 이건 물지 않아.

6. But I still don't like it. __________ it home. (*still: 여전히)
그래도 난 여전히 싫어. 그거 집에 가져오지 마.

CH 05

정답과 해설 p.11

Practice 2 명령문을 완성해 보아요.

다음 우리말 뜻과 같도록 주어진 표현을 순서에 맞게 배열하여 문장을 완성하세요.

1. (this question, Explain).
이 문제 좀 설명해줘. (*explain: 설명하다)

→ Explain this question.

2. (mistakes, be afraid of, Don't). 실수를 두려워하지 마세요.

→ ______________________.

3. (your, math textbooks, Open). 수학 교과서 펴세요.

→ ______________________.

4. (your, pencils, Take out). 연필을 꺼내세요.

→ ______________________.

5. (Tell, the answer, me) for the second question.
두 번째 문제의 답을 말해주세요.

→ ______________________ for the second question.

6. (a break, Take). 쉬세요.

→ ______________________.

7. (chocolate, some, Have). 초콜릿 좀 먹어.

→ ______________________.

정답과 해설 p.11

8. Wow, this is delicious. (another one, me, Give).
와, 이거 맛있다. 하나 더 주라.

➔ Wow, this is delicious. ______________________________.

9. (listen, Be quiet, and).
조용히 하고 들어보세요.

➔ ______________________.

10. (the volume, Raise).
음량을 높여줘.

➔ ______________________.

11. (your seats, Return to). 자리로 돌아가세요.

➔ ____.

12. (Don't, the volume, raise). 음량을 높이지 마.

➔ ____.

13. (your, recorders, Bring) for the next class.
다음 시간엔 리코더를 가져오세요.

➔ ______________________________ for the next class.

14. (Come to, house, my) after school. 학교 끝나고 우리 집으로 와.

➔ ______________________________ after school.

15. (me, bother, Don't). (*bother: 귀찮게 하다)
나를 귀찮게 하지 마.

➔ ____.

CH 05

정답과 해설 p.11

16. (prepared, Be) for anything. (*prepared: 준비가 된)
어떤 것에도 준비가 돼 있어야 해.

➔ ________________________________ for anything.

17. (the flowers, pick, Don't).
꽃을 꺾지 마세요.

➔ ________________________________.

18. (me, Tell, the truth).
나에게 진실을 말해줘.

➔ ________________________________.

19. (a circle, on the paper, Draw). 종이 위에 원을 하나 그리세요.

➔ ________________________________.

20. (your homework, Don't, forget). 숙제 잊지 마.

➔ ________________________________.

Cultural Tips
재미로 익히는 문화상식

다른 나라에서는 전화를 받을 때 어떻게 말할까요?

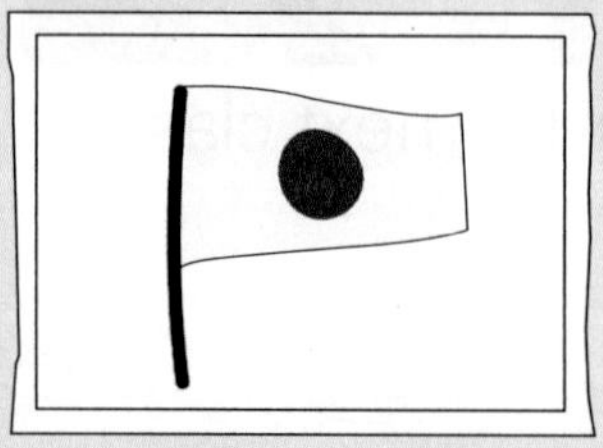

일본 - もしもし(모시모시)。

중국 - 喂(웨이)?

미국 - Hello(헬로우)?

프랑스 - Allô(알로)?

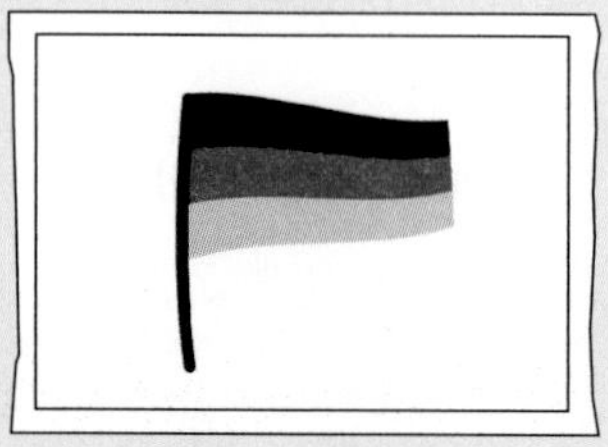

독일 - Hallo(할로)?

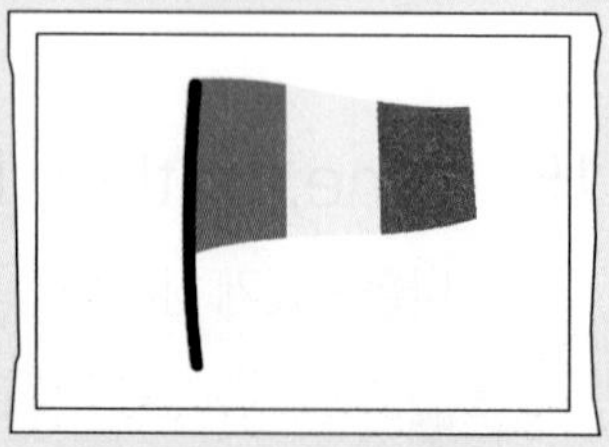

이탈리아 - Pronto(프론토)?

정답과 해설 p.11

Practice 3 명령문을 완성해 보아요.

다음 문장을 (　) 안의 지시에 따라 바꿔 보세요.

1. You make some brownies. (긍정 명령문으로)

➔ Make some brownies ______________________.

브라우니 좀 만들어줘.

2. You prepare the ingredients. (긍정 명령문으로)

➔ ______________________
______________________.

재료를 준비해.

3. You give me the recipe. (긍정 명령문으로)

➔ ______________________. 조리법을 나에게 (알려) 줘.

4. You write it down. (긍정 명령문으로)

➔ ______________________. 그것을 받아 적어.

5. You talk so fast. (부정 명령문으로)

➔ ______________________. 너무 빠르게 말하지 마.

6. You put flour in a bowl. (긍정 명령문으로)

➔ ______________________. 밀가루를 그릇에 넣어.

7. You add milk and eggs. (긍정 명령문으로)

➔ ______________________. 우유와 계란을 추가해(넣어).

정답과 해설 p.11

8. You bring some butter and sugar. (긍정 명령문으로)

➔ ____.

약간의 버터와 설탕을 가져와.

9. You mix them well. (긍정 명령문으로)

➔ ____. 그것들을 잘 섞어.

10. You mix too hard. (부정 명령문으로)

➔ ____. 너무 세게 섞지는 마.

11. You put it in the oven. (긍정 명령문으로)

➔ ____.

그것을 오븐에 넣어.

12. You wait for 10 minutes. (긍정 명령문으로)

➔ ____. 10분 기다려.

13. You are careful. (긍정 명령문으로)

➔ ____. 조심해.

14. You go to the supermarket. (긍정 명령문으로)

➔ ____. 슈퍼마켓에 가.

15. You buy any. (부정 명령문으로)

➔ ____. 아무것도 사지 마.

16. You ask me anything. (긍정 명령문으로)

➔ ____. 뭐든 나한테 물어봐.

정답과 해설 p.12

17. You worry too much.
(부정 명령문으로)

➔ ______________________________
______________________________.

너무 걱정하지 마.

18. You leave the kitchen.
(부정 명령문으로)

➔ ______________________________
______________________________.

부엌을 떠나지 마.

19. You forget the recipe! (부정 명령문으로)

➔ ____! 조리법 잊어버리지 마!

20. You clean the kitchen. (긍정 명령문으로)

➔ ____. 부엌을 청소해.

Cultural Tips
재미로 익히는
문화상식

마트료시카(Matryoshka) - 러시아의 전통 인형

"인형 안에서 또 인형이 나와!"
마트료시카는 큰 인형 안에 그것보다 작은 인형, 그리고 더 작은 인형을 여러 개 넣을 수 있게 만든 인형이에요.
인형을 품고 있는 모습이 알을 감싼 모습 같다고 해서 '마트료시카'(Matryoshka)란 이름 대신,
'알을 품은 인형'(nesting doll)으로 불리기도 해요.
인형이 무려 72개가 들어간 마트료시카도 만들어졌다고 하니 정말 대단하죠?

정답과 해설 p.12

Let's Practice More!

SET 01

학습목표 1 | **명령문의 모양을 익혀 보아요.** 공부한 날 : 맞은 개수 : /12개

다음 우리말 해석을 보고 ( ) 안에서 알맞은 것을 고르세요.

01. (Put / Puts) your books away. 여러분의 책들을 치우세요.

02. (Solve / Solves) the problems. 문제를 푸세요.

03. (Doesn't / Don't) speak during the exam. 시험 중에는 얘기하지 마세요.

04. (Be / Is) careful because it is hot. 뜨거우니까 조심하세요.

05. (Checks / Check) your bag. 가방 확인해보렴.

06. (Don't / Doesn't) worry, Mom. 걱정하지 마세요, 엄마.

07. (Gets / Get) in the car. 차에 타렴.

08. (Looks / Look) at this! 이거 봐!

09. (Is / Be) quiet and listen. 조용히 하고 들어보세요.

10. (Raise / Raises) the volume. 음량을 높여줘.

11. (Don't / Doesn't) bother me. 나를 귀찮게 하지 마.

12. (Tells / Tell) me the truth. 나에게 진실을 말해줘.

정답과 해설 p.12

Let's Practice More!

SET 02

학습목표 1 | **명령문의 모양을 익혀 보아요.** 공부한 날 : 맞은 개수 : /14개

다음 문장을 보고 올바른 명령문 모양이면 ○표, 틀리면 ×표 하세요.

01. Return to your seats. → ○
자리로 돌아가세요.

02. Don't raise the volume. → ______
음량을 높이지 마.

03. Brings your recorders for the next class. → ______
다음 시간엔 리코더를 가져오세요.

04. Comes to my house after school. → ______
학교 끝나고 우리 집으로 와.

05. Are prepared for anything. → ______
어떤 것에도 준비가 돼 있어야 해.

06. Don't pick the flowers. → ______
꽃을 꺾지 마세요.

07. Give the recipe to me. → ______
조리법을 나에게 (알려)줘.

08. Takes out a notebook. → ______
노트를 꺼내.

09. Mixes eggs, butter and sugar in a separate bowl. → ______
다른 그릇에 계란, 버터 그리고 설탕을 섞어.

10. Don't mix too hard. → ______
너무 세게 섞지는 마.

11. Be careful. → ______
조심해.

12. Goes to the supermarket tomorrow. → ______
내일 슈퍼마켓에 가.

13. Asks me. → ______
나한테 물어봐.

14. Finally, cleans the kitchen. → ______
마지막으로, 부엌을 청소해.

정답과 해설 p.12

Let's Practice More!

SET 03

학습목표 1 | **명령문의 모양을 익혀 보아요.** 공부한 날 : 맞은 개수 : /10개

우리말 뜻과 같도록 주어진 표현을 순서에 맞게 배열해 보세요.

01. (for / 10 minutes / Wait). 10분 기다려.

➔ Wait for 10 minutes.

02. (Come / house / my / to). 우리 집으로 와.

➔ ______________________.

03. (worry / Don't). 걱정하지 마.

➔ ______________________.

04. (Cook / 5 minutes / for). 5분 동안 익히세요.

➔ ______________________.

05. (textbooks / your / Open / math). 수학 교과서를 펴세요.

➔ ______________________.

06. (and / Be / listen / quiet). 조용히 하고 들어보세요.

➔ ______________________.

07. (Don't / homework / forget / your). 숙제 잊지 마.

➔ ______________________.

08. (for / brownies / Make / some / me).
나를 위해 브라우니 좀 만들어줘.

➔ ______________________.

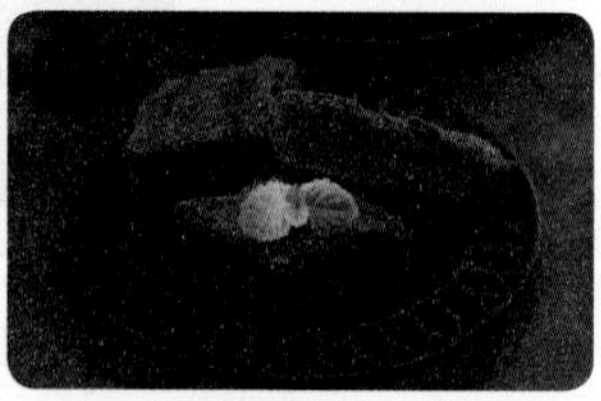

09. (leave / kitchen / Don't / the). 부엌을 떠나지 마.

➔ ______________________.

10. (paper / Draw / on / the / a circle). 종이 위에 원을 하나 그리세요.

➔ ______________________.

정답과 해설 p.12

Let's Practice More!

SET 04

학습목표 1 | **명령문의 모양을 익혀 보아요.** 공부한 날 : 맞은 개수 : /12개

다음 밑줄 친 표현이 맞으면 ○표, 틀리면 고쳐 써 보세요.

01. Boiling water until it gets hot. → Boil
물이 뜨거워질 때까지 끓이세요.

02. Put noodles and sauce into the pot. → ________
면과 소스를 냄비에 넣으세요.

03. Watch out for strangers. → ________
모르는 사람들을 조심해라.

04. Driving me to school. → ________
학교까지 태워다주세요.

05. Don't being afraid. → ________
무서워하지 마.

06. Don't bringing it home. → ________
그것을 집에 가져오지 마.

07. Explain this question. → ________
이 문제 좀 설명해줘.

08. Takes a break. → ________
쉬세요.

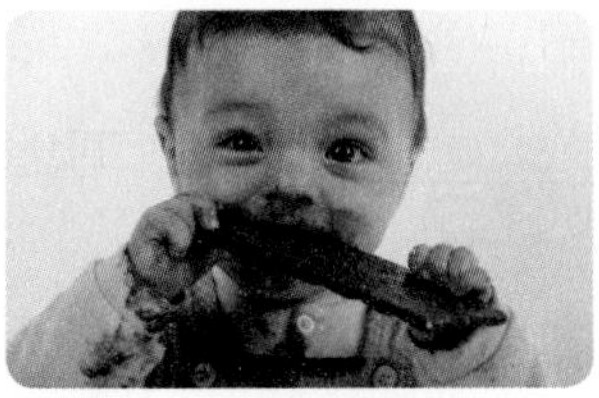

09. Have some chocolate. → ________
초콜릿 좀 먹어.

10. Gives me some chocolate. → ________
초콜릿 좀 줘.

11. Don't talk so fast. → ________
너무 빠르게 말하지 마.

12. Don't mixing too hard. → ________
너무 세게 섞지는 마.

정답과 해설 p.12

Let's Practice More!

SET 05

학습목표 1 | **명령문의 모양을 익혀 보아요.** 공부한 날 : 맞은 개수 : /10개

다음 문장을 긍정 명령문으로 바꿔 보세요.

01. You are careful.

➔ Be careful ______. 조심해.

02. You buy it.

➔ ______. 그것을 사.

03. You wait for 10 minutes.

➔ ______. 10분 동안 기다려.

04. You solve the problems.

➔ ______. 문제를 풀어.

05. You cook for 5 minutes.

➔ ______. 5분 동안 익혀.

06. You come here!

➔ ______! 이리 와!

07. You put it away.

➔ ______. 그것을 치워.

08. You take out your pencils.

➔ ______. 너의 연필들을 꺼내.

09. You explain this question.

➔ ______. 이 문제를 설명해줘.

10. You go to the supermarket tomorrow.

➔ ______. 내일 슈퍼마켓에 가.

정답과 해설 p.12

Let's Practice More!

SET 06

학습목표 2 | 긍정 명령문과 부정 명령문을 비교해 보아요. 공부한 날 : 맞은 개수 : /14개

다음 문장을 보고 밑줄 친 부분의 올바른 우리말 해석을 골라 보세요.

01. Ask me. (물어보세요 / 물어보지 마세요)

02. Don't worry. (걱정하세요 / 걱정하지 마세요)

03. Don't leave the kitchen. (떠나 / 떠나지 마)

04. Be careful because it is hot. (조심하지 마세요 / 조심하세요)

05. Check your bag. (확인하지 마 / 확인해봐)

06. Don't bring it home. (가져와 / 가져오지 마)

07. Don't be afraid of mistakes. (두려워하지 마세요 / 두려워하세요)

08. Raise the volume. (높이지 마 / 높여줘)

09. Don't talk so fast. (말해 / 말하지 마)

10. Come to my house. (오지 마 / 와)

11. Don't buy it. (사 / 사지 마)

12. Don't forget the recipe! (잊어버리지 마 / 잊어버려)

13. Drive me to school. (태워다 주지 마세요 / 태워다 주세요)

14. Don't speak during the exam. (얘기하세요 / 얘기하지 마세요)

정답과 해설 p.12

Let's Practice More!

SET 07

학습목표 2 | 긍정 명령문과 부정 명령문을 비교해 보아요. 공부한 날 : 맞은 개수 : /20개

다음 긍정 명령문을 부정 명령문으로 바꿔 보세요.

01. Forget the recipe!

➔ Don't forget the recipe!

그 조리법을 잊지 마!

02. Raise the volume.

➔ ______________________.

음량을 높이지 마.

03. Bother me.

➔ ______________________.

나를 귀찮게 하지 마.

04. Pick the flowers.

➔ ______________________.

꽃을 꺾지 마.

05. Forget your homework.

➔ ______________________.

너의 숙제를 잊지 마.

06. Get in the car.

➔ ______________________.

차에 타지 마.

07. Be afraid of mistakes.

➔ ______________________.

실수를 두려워하지 마.

08. Come here!

➔ ______________________!

이리 오지 마!

09. Take out your pencils.

➔ ______________________.

너의 연필들을 꺼내지 마.

정답과 해설 p.12

10. Take a break.

➔ ______________________________.

휴식을 취하지 마.

11. Return to your seats.

➔ ______________________________.

자리로 돌아가지 마.

12. Clean the kitchen.

➔ ______________________________.

부엌을 청소하지 마.

13. Mark your answers with a black pen.

➔ ______________________________.

너의 답을 검정색 펜으로 표시하지 마.

14. Speak during the exam.

➔ ______________________________.

시험을 치는 동안 얘기하지 마.

15. Put noodles and sauce into the pot.

➔ ______________________________.

면과 소스를 냄비에 넣지 마.

16. Open your math textbooks.

➔ ______________________________.

수학 교과서를 펴지 마.

17. Tell me the answer for the second question.

➔ ______________________________.

두 번째 문제에 대한 답을 나에게 말하지 마.

18. Bring your recorders for the next class.

➔ ______________________________.

너의 리코더를 다음 수업시간에 가져 오지 마.

19. Come to my house after school.

➔ ______________________________.

방과 후에 나의 집에 오지 마.

20. Talk so fast.

➔ ______________________________.

너무 빨리 말하지 마.

정답과 해설 p.13

Let's Practice More!

SET 08

학습목표 2 | 긍정 명령문과 부정 명령문을 비교해 보아요. 공부한 날 : 맞은 개수 : /20개

( ) 안의 지시대로 문장을 바꿔 보세요.

01. Don't put your books away. (긍정 명령문으로)

➔ Put your books away.

너의 책들을 치워.

02. Don't wait until the time is up. (긍정 명령문으로)

➔ ______________________.

시간이 다 될 때까지 기다려.

03. Draw a circle on the paper. (부정 명령문으로)

➔ ______________________.

그 종이에 원을 그리지 마.

04. Don't give me the recipe. (긍정 명령문으로)

➔ ______________________.

나에게 조리법을 (알려) 줘.

05. Mix too hard. (부정 명령문으로)

➔ ______________________.

너무 세게 섞지 마.

06. Don't stop yelling. (긍정 명령문으로)

➔ ______________________.

소리를 지르는 것을 멈춰.

07. Don't tell me the truth. (긍정 명령문으로)

➔ ______________________.

나에게 진실을 말해 줘.

08. Buy it. (부정 명령문으로)

➔ ______________________.

그것을 사지 마.

09. Don't add milk and eggs. (긍정 명령문으로)

➔ ______________________.

우유와 계란을 추가해(넣어).

정답과 해설 p.13

10. Don't watch out for strangers. (긍정 명령문으로)

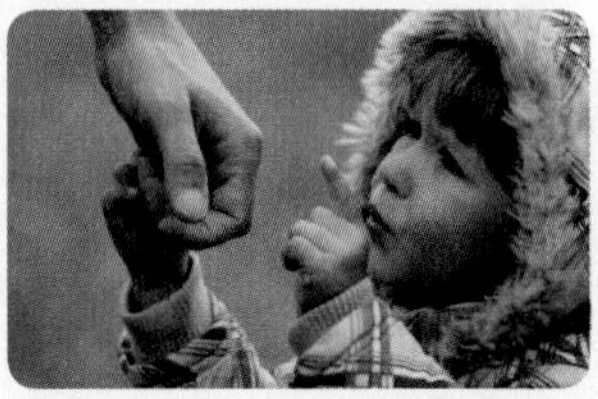

➔ ______________________________.

낯선 사람들을 조심해.

11. Look at this! (부정 명령문으로)

➔ ______________________________!

이것을 보지 마!

12. Don't put it away. (긍정 명령문으로)

➔ ______________________________.

그것을 치워.

13. Be afraid. (부정 명령문으로)

➔ ______________________________.

두려워하지 마.

14. Bring it home. (부정 명령문으로)

➔ ______________________________.

그것을 집으로 가져오지 마.

15. Don't be prepared for anything. (긍정 명령문으로)

➔ ______________________________.

어떤 것에도 준비가 돼 있어야 해.

16. Leave the kitchen. (부정 명령문으로)

➔ ______________________________.

부엌을 떠나지 마.

17. Don't come to my house. (긍정 명령문으로)

➔ ______________________________.

우리 집으로 와.

18. Forget the recipe! (부정 명령문으로)

➔ ______________________________!

조리법을 잊지 마!

19. Don't bring some butter and sugar. (긍정 명령문으로)

➔ ______________________________.

버터와 설탕 조금을 가져와.

20. Don't take out a notebook. (긍정 명령문으로)

➔ ______________________________.

공책을 꺼내.

정답과 해설 p.13

Chapter 06 청유문

이 챕터에서는 말하는 이가 듣는 이에게 제안하거나 요청할 때 쓰는 문장인 '청유문'에 대해 배워 보아요.

☆ 학습 방향 및 배울 내용 미리보기 ☆

☐ **Unit 01 : Let's do** it together!

청유문

청유문의 의미와 청유문을 만드는 방법에 대해 알아보아요.

▼

☐ **Unit 02 : How about going** to the movies?

제안을 나타내는 다른 표현

청유문의 다양한 표현들에 대해 알아보아요.

단어 미리보기

이 챕터에 나올 단어들 중 이미 알고 있는 단어가 있나요?
맞는 뜻을 골라 체크해 봐요.

날짜 : 이름 : 알고 있는 단어의 수 : /24개

No.	아는 단어	단어	품사	알맞은 뜻에 체크 표시해 봐요.			
1	☑	inside	부사	밖으로	☐	안으로	☑
2	☐	order	동사	주문하다	☐	질문하다	☐
3	☐	fried	형용사	삶은	☐	기름에 튀긴	☐
4	☐	worry	동사	걱정하다	☐	관심이 없다	☐
5	☐	fight	동사	싸우다	☐	화해하다	☐
6	☐	bread	명사	밀가루	☐	빵	☐
7	☐	poor	형용사	불쌍한	☐	돈 많은	☐
8	☐	plan	명사	계획	☐	땅	☐
9	☐	travel	동사	운전하다	☐	여행하다	☐
10	☐	island	명사	섬	☐	도시	☐
11	☐	busy	형용사	한가한	☐	바쁜	☐
12	☐	start	동사	시작하다	☐	끝내다	☐
13	☐	idea	명사	생각	☐	잠	☐
14	☐	need	동사	주다	☐	필요로 하다	☐
15	☐	ride	동사	걷다	☐	(탈것을) 타다	☐
16	☐	rest	명사	화장실	☐	휴식	☐
17	☐	spend	동사	(시간을) 보내다	☐	벌다	☐
18	☐	meet	동사	헤어지다	☐	만나다	☐
19	☐	choose	동사	버리다	☐	선택하다	☐
20	☐	river	명사	산	☐	강	☐
21	☐	outside	부사	안으로	☐	밖으로	☐
22	☐	check	동사	확인하다	☐	의심하다	☐
23	☐	enough	형용사	부족한	☐	충분한	☐
24	☐	paint	동사	(그림을) 그리다	☐	기절하다	☐

UNIT 청유문

01 Let's do it together!

❖ POiNT 1 ❖

청유문은 '(우리) ~하자/하지 말자'라고 제안하거나 요청하는 문장이에요.

명령문 Go to the park. (너) 공원에 가라.

청유문 Let's go to the park. (우리) 공원에 가자.

❖ POiNT 2 ❖

청유문 만들기

'~하자'라고 제안할 때는 Let's+동사원형**을 쓰고, '~하지 말자'라고 제안할 때는** Let's not+동사원형**으로 표현해요. 'Let's'는 'Let us'의 줄임말이랍니다.**

Let's+동사원형 ~하자	**Let's go** inside. 안으로 들어가자. **Let's take** a break. 잠깐 쉬자. **Let's order** fried chicken. 프라이드 치킨을 주문하자. **Let's do** it together! 우리 같이 그걸 하자!
Let's not+동사원형 ~하지 말자	**Let's not** waste time. We have a lot of homework. 시간 낭비하지 말자. 우리는 숙제가 많이 있어. **Let's not** fight. 싸우지 말자. **Let's not** worry about it. 그것에 대해 걱정하지 말자.

Check and Write

Let's나 Let's not을 이용하여 빈칸을 알맞게 채워보세요.

1. [Let's] paint together!
함께 그림을 그리자!

2. [   ] take a picture!
사진 찍자!

3. [   ] mess up the room!
방을 어지럽히지 말자!

4. [   ] fight!
싸우지 말자!

5. [   ] dance.
춤추자.

정답과 해설 p.13

UNIT 02

제안을 나타내는 다른 표현

How about going to the movies?

제안을 나타내는 다른 표현에는 'How about~?', 'Why don't you[we]~?', 'Why not~?'이 있고, '~하는 게 어때?'라고 해석해요!

❖ POiNT 1 ❖

How about + –ing~?

How about going to the movies?

영화 보러 가는 게 어때?

How about playing games?

게임 하는 게 어때?

❖ POiNT 2 ❖

Why don't you[we] + 동사원형~?

Why don't you get some sleep?
You look tired.

좀 자는 게 어때? 너 피곤해 보여.

Why don't we eat out?

우리 외식하는 게 어때?

❖ POiNT 3 ❖

Why not + 동사원형~?

Why not take a break?

잠깐 쉬는 게 어때?

Why not bring the poor puppy home?

그 불쌍한 강아지를 집으로 데려오는 게 어때?

Check and Write

우리말 해석에 맞도록 보기 에서 알맞은 것을 골라 빈칸을 채워보세요.

보기 not don't about sing making

1. How [about] eating pizza?
피자를 먹는 게 어때?

2. Why don't you [ ]?
너 노래하는 게 어때?

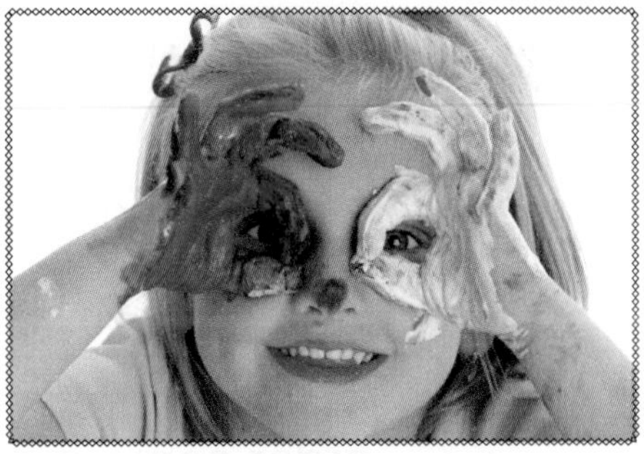

3. Why [ ] wash your hands?
손을 씻는 게 어때?

4. How about [ ] bread together?
같이 빵을 만드는 게 어때?

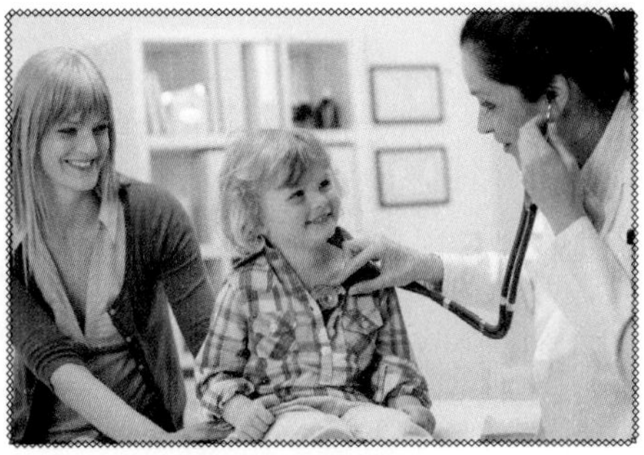

5. Why [ ] you see a doctor?
의사에게 진찰을 받는 게 어때?

정답과 해설 p.13

Practice 1 제안하거나 요청하는 청유형 문장을 익혀 보아요.

주어진 우리말 뜻과 같도록 보기 에서 알맞은 표현을 골라 빈칸에 써 보세요.

A Family trip

보기 Let's How about Let's not Why not

1. ___How___ ___about___ traveling to Jeju Island?
제주도로 여행을 가면 어떨까?

2. Sounds great. __________ make a plan.
좋아. 계획을 짜보자.

3. __________ __________ go to Jeju Island tomorrow?
내일 제주도에 가는 게 어때?

4. __________ __________ hurry. We have enough time. (*enough: 충분한)
서두르지 말자. 시간은 충분히 있어.

B Let's eat out!

보기 Why don't you Let's Let's not put How about

1. __________ __________ __________
order some pizza? 피자를 좀 주문하는 건 어때?

2. I don't like pizza. __________ __________
eating out? 나는 피자 싫어. 외식하는 건 어때?

3. Okay, __________ your coat on. 좋아, 코트 입어.

4. I will. __________ go to a Chinese restaurant.
그럴게. 중식당 가자.

5. Sure. __________ __________ fight about the menu.
그래. 메뉴로 다투지 말자.

정답과 해설 p.13

C Shopping time

보기 Let's Why don't we How about Let's not

1. Mom! __________ go shopping together. 엄마! 같이 쇼핑가요.

2. __________ __________ going to the mall with your sister?
   누나랑 같이 쇼핑몰에 가는 건 어때?
   She needs new clothes. 그녀는 새 옷이 필요해.

3. She is busy today. 오늘 그녀는 바빠요.
   __________ __________ __________ buy new clothes for her?
   우리가 그녀를 위해서 새 옷을 사는 것은 어때요?

4. Okay. __________ __________ waste time. 그래. 시간 낭비하지 말자.

D Movie night

보기 watch How about buy Let's not Why not Why don't we

1. __________ __________ go to a movie together?
   같이 영화 보러 갈까?

2. That is a great idea. 좋은 생각이야.
   But, let's not __________ an action movie. 하지만 액션영화는 보지 말자.

3. __________ __________ __________ watch a horror movie?
   우리 공포영화 보는 게 어때?

4. I don't want to have a nightmare. 나는 악몽을 꾸고 싶지 않아.
   __________ __________ watching "The Jungle Book"?
   '정글북'을 보는 건 어때?

5. Sounds good. Let's __________ tickets. The movie starts at 6 o'clock. 좋아. 표를 사자. 영화는 6시에 시작해.

6. __________ __________ be late. 늦지 말자.

정답과 해설 p.13

Practice 2 제안하거나 요청하는 청유형 문장을 완성해 보아요.

다음 우리말 뜻과 같도록 주어진 표현을 순서에 맞게 배열하여 문장을 완성하세요.

1. *Suhyun* : I am so tired. 너무 피곤하다.
   Jiyeon : (take a break, you, Why don't)? 잠깐 쉬는 게 어때?
   ➔ *Jiyeon* : Why don't you take a break ____________?

2. No! The weather is nice. (go, Let's, to the park) and play.
   안 돼! 날씨가 좋아. 공원에 가서 놀자.
   ➔ No! The weather is nice. ____________________ and play.

3. (this red skirt, not, wear, Why)? 이 빨간 치마를 입는 건 어때?
   ➔ ______________________________?

4. (not, wear skirts, Let's). We have to run around.
   치마는 입지 말자. 우리는 뛰어놀아야 해.
   ➔ ______________________________. We have to run around.

5. (clean your room, Why don't you)? 네 방을 좀 치우는 건 어때?
   ➔ ____?

6. (clean, the room, Let's) later. 나중에 방을 치우자.
   ➔ ______________________________ later.

7. (about, playing soccer, How) at the park? 공원에서 축구를 하는 건 어때?
   ➔ ______________________________ at the park?

8. That's a good idea. (not, waste time, Let's). 좋은 생각이야. 시간을 낭비하지 말자.
   ➔ That's a good idea. ______________________________.

9. (not, go home, Why) for dinner? 저녁 먹으러 집으로 가는 게 어때?
   ➔ ______________________________ for dinner?

10. I am hungry. (a bus, take, Let's). 나 배고파. 버스 타자.
    ➔ I am hungry. ______________________________.

정답과 해설 p.13

11. But your house is near. (home, walk, Why don't you)?
하지만 너희 집은 가깝잖아. 걸어서 집에 가는 건 어때?

➔ But your house is near. ______________________________?

12. Ok. (go, on foot, Let's). (*on foot: 걸어서, 도보로)
그래. 걸어서 가자.

➔ Ok. ______________________________.

13. (not, leave anything, Let's). 아무것도 두고 가지 말자.

➔ ______________________________.

14. I love soccer. (about, coming back, How) tomorrow?
나는 축구가 너무 좋아. 내일도 또 오는 건 어때?

➔ I love soccer. ______________________________ tomorrow?

15. (a museum, Let's, visit). 박물관에 가자.

➔ ______________________________.

16. (go back, Why don't you, to your house)? 너희 집으로 돌아가는 건 어때?

➔ ______________________________?

17. (a game, Let's, play).
게임 하나 하자.

➔ ______________________________.

18. (Why, take a picture, not)?
사진을 한 장 찍는 건 어떨까?

➔ ______________________________?

19. (stay, Why don't you, with us)? 우리랑 같이 있는 건 어때?

➔ ______________________________?

20. (a present, Let's, buy) for Mom. 엄마를 위한 선물을 하나 사자.

➔ ______________________________ for Mom.

정답과 해설 p.14

Practice 3 제안하거나 요청하는 청유형 문장을 써 보아요.

[1 – 15] 우리말 뜻을 참고하여 다음 주어진 표현을 활용해 문장을 완성해 보세요.
(필요한 경우 주어진 동사의 형태를 변형해서 쓰세요.)

1. (Let's, ride, a bike)
자전거를 타자.

→ Let's ride a bike.

2. (Why not, watch a movie)
영화를 보는 건 어때?

→ ______________________?

3. (Why don't you, check the weather) 날씨를 확인해 보는 게 어때?
→ ______________________________________?

4. (Let's not, go outside) 내일 비가 올 테니 밖에 나가지 말자.
→ It will rain tomorrow, so ______________________.

5. (How about, go to, the Han River) 한강 가는 거 어때?
→ ______________________________________?

6. (Let's, do, something different) 무언가 다른 걸 하자.
→ ______________________________________.

7. (Why don't you, choose the menu) 네가 메뉴를 정하는 건 어때?
→ ______________________________________?

정답과 해설 p.14

8. (How about, order some pizza) 좋아. 저녁으로 피자를 좀 주문하는 건 어때?

➔ Great. ______________________________ for dinner?

9. (Let's not, have it) 나는 피자 안 좋아해, 그러니까 그거 먹지 말자.

➔ I don't like pizza, so ______________________________.

10. (How about, play video games)

비디오 게임을 하는 건 어때?

➔ ______________________________

______________________________?

11. (Why not, eat out)

외식할까?

➔ ______________________________

______________________________?

12. (Let's, go to, the Thai restaurant) 태국 음식점에 가자.

➔ ______________________________.

13. (Why don't you, get some rest) 이제 쉬는 게 어때?

➔ ______________________________ now?

14. (How about, meet, at 5 o'clock) 5시에 만나는 건 어때?

➔ ______________________________?

15. (Let's not, forget, our plan) 우리의 계획을 잊지 말자.

➔ ______________________________.

CH 06

정답과 해설 p.14

[16 – 20] 다음 문장을 읽고 알맞은 해석을 고르세요.

16. Why not go on a picnic?

(*go on a picnic: 소풍을 가다)

➔ (소풍 가는 건 어때? / 소풍을 안 가면 어때?)

17. Why don't you go to the park tomorrow?

➔ (너 내일 공원에 가는 건 어떠니? / 너는 내일 공원에 안 가면 어떠니?)

18. Now let's forget this mistake.

➔ (이제 이 실수를 잊어버려라. / 이제 이 실수를 잊어버리자.)

19. Let's play at Suhyun's house.

➔ (수현이네 집에서 놀아라. / 수현이네 집에서 놀자.)

20. How about spending time with your family?

➔ (가족과 함께 시간을 보내는 건 어때? / 가족과 함께 시간을 보냈니?)

정답과 해설 p.14

Let's Practice More!

SET 01

학습목표 1 | Let's와 Let's not을 익혀 보아요. 공부한 날 : 맞은 개수 : /12개

다음 청유문을 읽고 밑줄 친 부분이 맞으면 ○표, 틀리면 바르게 고쳐 보세요.

01. Let's buying a present for mom. → buy
엄마를 위한 선물을 사자.

02. Let's ride a bike. → ______
자전거를 타자.

03. Let's not eat it. → ______
먹지 말자.

04. Let's does something different. → ______
무언가 다른 것을 하자.

05. Let's go to the Thai restaurant. → ______
태국 음식점에 가자.

06. Let's forget not our plan. → ______
우리의 계획을 잊지 말자.

07. Let's not worry about it. → ______
그건 걱정하지 말자.

08. Let's making a plan. → ______
계획을 세우자.

09. Let's don't waste time. → ______
시간을 낭비하지 말자.

10. Let's not wear skirts. → ______
치마는 입지 말자.

11. Let's go to the park and play. → ______
공원에 가서 놀자.

12. Let's cleaned the room later. → ______
방은 나중에 청소하자.

CH 06

정답과 해설 p.14

Let's Practice More!

SET 02

학습목표 1 | Let's와 Let's not을 익혀 보아요.　　공부한 날 :　　맞은 개수 :　　/14개

다음 우리말 뜻을 보고 주어진 문장을 Let's 또는 Let's not을 이용해 제안하는 문장으로 바꿔 보세요.

01. 

We take a bus.

→ Let's take a bus.

버스 타자.

02. 

We play at Mina's house.

→ ____________________

____________________.

미나네 집에서 놀자.

03. We go together.

→ ____________________.

함께 가자.

04. We don't leave anything.

→ ____________________.

아무것도 두고 가지 말자.

05. We visit a museum.

→ ____________________.

박물관에 가자.

06. We are not late.

→ ____________________.

늦지 말자.

정답과 해설 p.14

07. We forget this mistake.

➔ ____.

이 실수를 잊어버리자.

08. We don't hurry.

➔ ____.

서두르지 말자.

09. We don't fight about the menu.

➔ ____.

메뉴로 다투지 말자.

10. We go on foot.

➔ ______________________________. 걸어서 가자.

11. We don't watch an action movie.

➔ ____.

액션영화는 보지 말자.

12. We play a game.

➔ ______________________________. 게임 하자.

13. We buy tickets.

➔ ____.

표를 사자.

14. We don't go outside.

➔ ______________________________. 밖에 나가지 말자.

정답과 해설 p.14

Let's Practice More!

SET 03

학습목표 2 | Why not, Why don't you, How about을 구분해 보아요. 공부한 날 : 맞은 개수 : /14개

다음 빈칸에 How와 Why 중 알맞은 것을 골라 써 보세요.

01. ___How___ about traveling to Jeju Island? 제주도로 여행을 가는 게 어때?

02. ________ not go to Jeju Island tomorrow? 내일 제주도에 가는 게 어때?

03. ________ don't you order some pizza?
피자를 좀 주문하는 게 어때?

04. ________ about eating out? 외식하는 건 어때?

05. ________ don't you buy new clothes for her? 그녀를 위해서 새 옷을 사오는 건 어때요?

06. ________ not go to a movie together? 같이 영화를 보러 갈까?

07. ________ don't you watch a horror movie? 공포영화를 보는 게 어때?

08. ________ about going to the mall with your sister?
누나랑 같이 쇼핑몰에 가는 건 어때?

09. ________ don't you take a break?
잠깐 쉬는 게 어때?

10. ________ not wear this red skirt? 이 빨간 치마를 입는 게 어때?

11. ________ don't you walk home? 걸어서 집에 가는 건 어때?

12. ________ about coming back tomorrow? 내일도 또 오는 건 어때?

13. ________ about watching "The Jungle Book"?
'정글북'을 보는 게 어때?

14. ________ don't you clean your room?
네 방을 좀 치우는 건 어때?

정답과 해설 p.14

Let's Practice More!

SET 04

학습목표 2 | Why not, Why don't you, How about을 구분해 보아요. 공부한 날 : 맞은 개수 : /12개

Why don't you 제안문은 How about으로, How about 제안문은 Why don't you로 바꿔 보세요.

01. How about traveling to Jeju Island?
→ Why don't you travel to Jeju Island? 제주도로 여행을 가는 게 어때?

02. Why don't you order some pizza?
→ ____________________? 피자를 좀 주문하는 게 어때?

03. How about eating out?
→ ____________________?
외식하는 건 어때?

04. How about going to the mall with your sister?
→ ____________________?
언니랑 같이 쇼핑몰에 가는 건 어때?

05. Why don't you buy new clothes for her?
→ ____________________? 그녀를 위해서 새 옷을 사는 건 어때?

06. How about watching "The Jungle Book"?
→ ____________________? '정글북'을 보는 건 어때?

07. Why don't you take a break?
→ ____________________? 잠깐 쉬는 건 어때?

08. Why don't you clean your room?
→ ____________________? 네 방을 좀 치우는 건 어때?

09. How about playing soccer at the park?
→ ____________________? 공원에서 축구를 하는 건 어때?

10. Why don't you walk home?
→ ____________________? 걸어서 집에 가는 건 어때?

11. How about coming back tomorrow?
→ ____________________? 내일도 또 오는 건 어때?

12. Why don't you go back to your house?
→ ____________________? 너희 집으로 돌아가는 건 어때?

정답과 해설 p.14

Let's Practice More!

SET 05

학습목표 2 | Why not, Why don't you, How about을 구분해 보아요. 공부한 날 : 맞은 개수 : /14개

다음 우리말 뜻을 보고 주어진 표현들을 순서대로 바르게 배열해 보세요.

01. (go / Why not / Jeju Island / to / tomorrow)?
내일 제주도에 가는 게 어때?
→ Why not go to Jeju Island tomorrow ?

02. (Why not / a movie / together / to / go)?
같이 영화 보러 갈까?
→ ______ ?

03. (a horror movie / Why don't you / watch)?
공포영화 보는 게 어때?
→ ______ ?

04. (wear / Why not / this red skirt)?
이 빨간 치마를 입는 건 어때?
→ ______ ?

05. (the park / How about / soccer / playing / at)?
공원에서 축구를 하는 건 어때?
→ ______ ?

06. (go / home / Why not / for dinner)?
저녁 먹으러 집으로 가는 게 어때?
→ ______ ?

07. (Why don't you / your house / go back / to)?
너희 집으로 돌아가는 건 어때?
→ ______ ?

정답과 해설 p.15

08. (a picture / Why not / take)?

사진을 한 장 찍는 건 어때?

➔ ____?

09. (with / Why don't you / stay / us)?

우리랑 같이 있는 건 어때?

➔ ____?

10. (How about / to / going / the Han River)?

한강 가는 거 어때?

➔ ____?

CH 06

11. (check / Why don't you / the weather)?

날씨를 확인해 보는 게 어때?

➔ ____?

12. (a movie / watch / Why not)?

영화를 보는 건 어때?

➔ ____?

13. (playing / How about / video games)?

비디오 게임을 하는 건 어때?

➔ ____?

14. (ordering / How about / some pizza)?

피자를 좀 주문하는 건 어때?

➔ ____?

정답과 해설 p.15

Let's Practice More!

SET 06

학습목표 2 | Why not, Why don't you, How about을 구분해 보아요. 공부한 날 : 맞은 개수 : /14개

다음 문장에서 밑줄 친 부분이 맞으면 ○표, 틀리면 고쳐 써 보세요.

01. How about go to the movies? → going
영화를 보러 가는 게 어때?

02. Why don't you choose the menu? → ______
네가 메뉴를 정하는 건 어때?

03. Why not eating out? → ______
외식할까?

04. Why don't you getting some rest now? → ______
이제 쉬는 게 어때?

05. How about meet at 5 o'clock? → ______
5시에 만나는 건 어때?

06. Why not go on a picnic? → ______
소풍가는 건 어때?

07. Why don't you going to the park? → ______
공원에 가는 건 어때?

08. Why not going home for dinner? → ______
저녁 먹으러 집에 가는 게 어때?

09. Why not taking a picture? → ______
사진을 한 장 찍는 게 어때?

10. Why don't you staying with us? → ______
우리랑 같이 있는 건 어때?

11. How about going to the Han River? → ______
한강 가는 거 어때?

12. Why don't you checking the weather? → ______
날씨를 확인해 보는 게 어때?

13. Why not watching a movie? → ______
영화를 보는 건 어때?

14. How about play video games? → ______
비디오 게임을 하는 건 어때?

정답과 해설 p.15

Let's Practice More!

SET 07

학습목표 3 | 명령문과 청유문을 비교해 보아요. 공부한 날 : 맞은 개수 : /20개

다음 문장을 읽고 밑줄 친 부분의 알맞은 우리말 해석을 고르세요.

01. Let's make a plan. (짜 / 짜보자)

02. Don't go outside. (나가지마 / 나가지 말자)

03. Put on your coat. (입어 / 입자)

04. Let's go to a Chinese restaurant. (가 / 가자)

05. Let's not fight about the menu. (다투지마 / 다투지 말자)

06. Let's ride a bike. (타 / 타자)

07. Don't waste time. (낭비하지마 / 낭비하지 말자)

08. Let's not watch an action movie. (보지마 / 보지 말자)

09. Buy tickets. (사 / 사자)

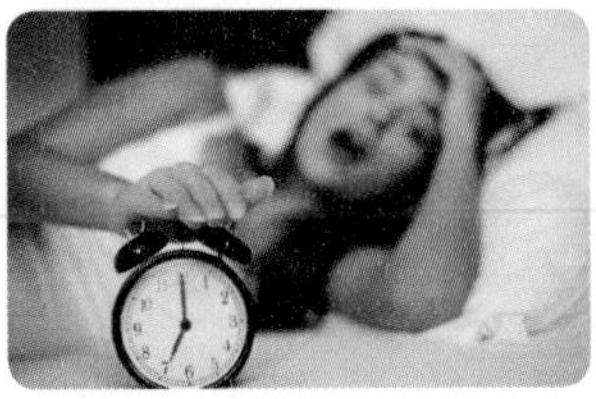

10. Let's not be late. (늦지마 / 늦지 말자)

11. Let's not eat it. (먹지마 / 먹지 말자)

12. Don't wear that skirt. (입지마 / 입지 말자)

13. Let's clean the room later. (치워 / 치우자)

14. Let's go together. (가 / 가자)

15. Let's take a bus. (타 / 타자)

16. Don't leave anything. (두고 가지마 / 두고 가지 말자)

17. Go on foot. (가 / 가자)

18. Let's visit a museum. (가 / 가자)

19. Play a game. (해 / 하자)

20. Let's buy a present for Mom. (사 / 사자)

정답과 해설 p.15

Let's Practice More!

SET 08

학습목표 4 | Why not, Why don't you, How about, Let's, Let's not을 이용해 청유문을 만들어 보아요.

공부한 날 : 맞은 개수 : /20개

( ) 안의 표현을 이용해서 주어진 문장을 청유문으로 바꿔 써 보세요.

01. You go to a Chinese restaurant.(Why not)

→ Why not go to a Chinese restaurant? 중식당에 가는 게 어때?

02. You do something different.(How about)

→ ____________________? 무언가 다른 걸 하는 게 어때?

03. You order some hamburgers.(How about)

→ ____________________?

햄버거를 좀 주문하는 게 어때?

04. You choose the menu.(Why don't you)

→ ____________________? 네가 메뉴를 정하는 건 어때?

05. You eat out.(Why not)

→ ____________________? 외식할까?

06. We go to the Thai restaurant.(Let's)

→ ____________________. 태국 음식점에 가자.

07. You go to the park.(Why don't you)

→ ____________________?

공원에 가는 게 어때?

08. We don't forget our plan.(Let's not)

→ ____________________. 우리의 계획을 잊지 말자.

09. You go on a picnic.(Why not)

→ ____________________? 소풍 가는 건 어때?

정답과 해설 p.15

10. We forget this mistake.(Let's)

➔ ______________________________________. 이 실수를 잊어버리자.

11. You get some rest now.(Why don't you)

➔ ______________________________________? 이제 쉬는 게 어때?

12. We play at Mina's house.(Let's)

➔ ______________________________________. 미나네 집에서 놀자.

13. You spend time with your family.(How about)

➔ ______________________________________?

너의 가족과 함께 시간을 보내는 건 어때?

14. We don't worry about it.(Let's not)

➔ ______________________________________. 그것에 대해 걱정하지 말자.

15. You wear this red coat.(Why not)

➔ ______________________________________?

이 빨간 코트를 입는 건 어때?

16. We don't waste time.(Let's not)

➔ ______________________________________. 시간 낭비하지 말자.

17. You watch a horror movie.(Why don't you)

➔ ______________________________________? 공포영화를 보는 게 어때?

18. You travel to France.(How about)

➔ ______________________________________? 프랑스로 여행을 가는 건 어때?

19. You play soccer at the park.(How about)

➔ ______________________________________? 공원에서 축구를 하는 건 어때?

20. We take a bus.(Let's)

➔ ______________________________________. 버스 타자.

정답과 해설 p.15

실전테스트 CHAPTER 04~06

공부한 날 :
복습한 날 :
부모님 확인 :

CHAPTER 04 감탄문 CHAPTER 05 명령문 CHAPTER 06 청유문

● 정답과 해설은 별책 15쪽에서 확인하세요!!

[01~02] 다음 문장의 빈칸에 How나 What 중 알맞은 것을 넣어 감탄문을 완성하세요.

01

_________ a high mountain!

02

_________ beautiful this garden is!

03

다음 빈칸에 들어갈 알맞은 말을 고르세요.

What _____________ ring this is!

① a expensive
② how expensive
③ the expensive
④ an expensive

04

다음 감탄문을 평서문으로 바꾸어 쓰세요.

How sick my brother is!

⇨ ______________________________

05

다음 단어들을 순서에 맞게 배열하여 문장을 완성하세요.

(an / house / this / What / old / is)!

⇨ ______________________________

06

우리말과 같도록 빈칸에 알맞은 말을 쓰세요.

_________ play the piano at night.
(밤에 피아노를 치지 말아라.)

07

다음 대화의 빈칸에 알맞은 말을 고르세요.

A: How's the weather today?
B: It's sunny and cool.
A: Wow! _________ play soccer.

① Do ② Don't
③ Let's ④ Can

08

다음 중 도서관에서 지켜야 할 규칙들로 적합한 것 두 개를 고르세요.

① Don't run.
② Don't be late.
③ Don't open your eyes.
④ Don't talk loudly.

[09~10] 다음 빈칸에 공통으로 들어갈 말을 쓰세요.

09 ________

A: ________ play baseball.
(야구하자.)
B: Sounds good! ________ have lunch first.
(좋아! 먼저 점심을 먹자.)

10 ________

A: ________ forget Mother's birthday!
(엄마의 생신을 잊지 마!)
B: Of course not. This is my present for her.
(물론이지. 이건 그녀를 위한 나의 선물이야.)
A: Wow! What is it?
(와! 뭐야?)
B: It's a secret. ________ touch the present.
(비밀이야. 선물을 만지지 마.)

[11~12] 다음 그림을 참고하여, 명령문을 완성하세요.

11

________ close the door.
(문을 닫아 주세요.)

12

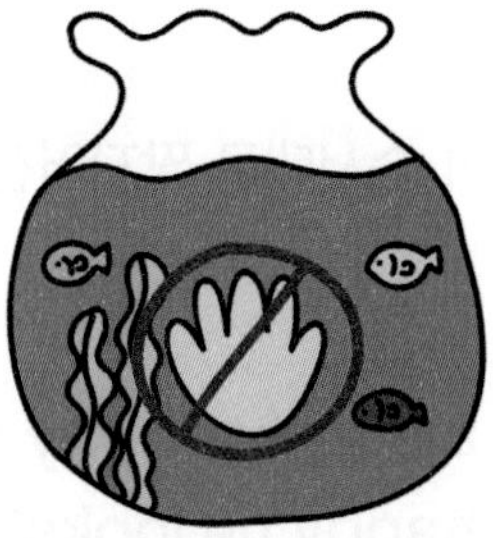

________ touch the fish.
(물고기를 만지지 마시오.)

13
다음 중 청유문을 고르세요.

① She has long hair.
② Let's take a walk.
③ You look cute.
④ Don't lie to me.

[14~15] 다음 괄호 안의 지시에 따라 주어진 문장을 바꿔 보세요.

14 (명령문으로)

You are a nice person.

____

15 (Let's 청유문으로)

We eat Japanese food.

____

실전테스트

16

빈칸에 알맞은 말이 순서대로 짝지어진 것을 고르세요.

> ________ a small country this is!
> ________ happy he looks!

① Who - What
② How - What
③ What - How
④ How - Why

17

다음 빈칸에 들어갈 수 <u>없는</u> 말을 고르세요.

> What a ________ girl Jane is!

① pretty
② happy
③ smart
④ nicely

18

다음 문장을 감탄문으로 바꾸어 쓰세요.

Mina sings very well.

⇨ ____________________

19

다음 밑줄 친 부분을 고쳐서 감탄문을 다시 쓰세요.

<u>How</u> old cars these are!

⇨ ____________________

20

다음 중 밑줄 친 부분이 어색한 것을 고르세요.

① <u>What</u> a happy man he is!
② <u>What</u> hot this tea is!
③ <u>How</u> brave the boy is!
④ <u>How</u> foolish the boys are!

[21~22] 다음 표현들을 순서에 맞게 배열하여 문장을 완성하세요.

21

> (your / lose / Don't / bag).

⇨ ____________________

22

> (not / it / see / Let's).

⇨ ____________________

23

다음 빈칸에 들어갈 수 <u>없는</u> 말을 고르세요.

> A: We must be quiet in the library.
> B: You're right. ________ run.

① Don't
② Never
③ Be
④ Let's not

[24~25] 다음 문장을 괄호 안의 지시에 따라 바꾸었을 때 옳지 않은 것을 고르세요.

24

① You turn up the volume. (긍정 명령문)
→ Turn up the volume.
② We listen to music. (청유문)
→ Let's listen to music.
③ You don't begin your speech. (부정 명령문)
→ Begin your speech.
④ We stay here tonight. (청유문)
→ Let's stay here tonight.

25

① We turn on the light. (청유문)
→ Let's turn on the light.
② You put the sign on the board. (명령문)
→ Put the sign on the board, please.
③ We bring this to her. (명령문)
→ Let's bring this to her.
④ You don't drink coffee. (부정 명령문)
→ Don't drink coffee.

26

다음 문장을 청유문으로 바르게 고친 것을 고르세요.

We eat the cookies.

① Did we eat the cookies?
② Do we eat the cookies?
③ Let's eat the cookies.
④ Eat the cookies.

27

다음 문장을 부정 명령문으로 바꿀 때 빈칸에 들어갈 알맞은 말을 고르세요.

You don't play computer games.
(넌 컴퓨터 게임을 하지 않는다.)
→ ________ play computer games.
(컴퓨터 게임을 하지 마세요.)

① No　② Do
③ Please　④ Don't

28

다음 문장을 긍정 명령문으로 바꿀 때 빈칸에 들어갈 알맞은 말을 고르세요.

You exercise today.
(넌 오늘 운동을 한다.)
→ ________ exercise today.
(오늘은 운동을 하세요.)

① Does　② Did
③ Please　④ Never

[29~30] 우리말 해석과 같도록 빈칸에 들어갈 알맞은 단어를 쓰세요.

29

________ ________ eating out?
(외식하는 게 어때?)

30

________ ________ go home?
(집에 가는 게 어때?)

Cultural Tips

재미로 익히는 문화상식

귀여운 강아지들의 국적을 알아볼까요?

이름 : 시츄 (Shih Tzu)
국적 : 중국

이름 : 요크셔 테리어
(Yorkshire Terrier)
국적 : 영국

이름 : 포메라니안
(Pomeranian)
국적 : 독일

이름 : 말티즈 (Maltese)
국적 : 이탈리아

이름 : 비숑 프리제
(Bichon Frise)
국적 : 벨기에, 프랑스

이름 : 치와와 (Chihuahua)
국적 : 멕시코

귀여운 고양이들의 국적을 알아볼까요?

이름 : 터키시 앙고라
(Turkish Angora)
국적 : 튀르키예

이름 : 샤미즈, 샴
(Siamese)
국적 : 태국

이름 : 노르웨이 숲 고양이
(Norwegian Forest Cat)
국적 : 노르웨이

이름 : 러시안 블루
(Russian Blue)
국적 : 러시아

이름 : 페르시안
(Persian)
국적 : 페르시아

이름 : 아메리칸 숏헤어
(American Shorthair)
국적 : 미국

초등영문법3800제 LEVEL 3

워크북

WORKBOOK

1. **단어 쓰기 연습** mp3 음성 파일을 듣고 들려주는 단어를 세 번씩 써 보아요.
2. **Dictation Test** mp3 음성 파일을 듣고 빈칸을 채워 보세요.
3. **단어테스트** 단어 쓰기 연습을 하며 암기한 단어들을 제대로 외웠는지 확인해 보아요.
4. **워크북 정답** Dictation Test와 단어테스트의 정답

초등영문법3800제 MP3 파일 이용 방법

1. 홈페이지에서 다운로드

① 마더텅 홈페이지(www.toptutor.co.kr) 접속 → 상단 메뉴 중 [초등 · 유아]의 [교재 소개] 선택
→ 교재 목록에서 해당 교재명 찾아 선택 → 학습자료의 [mp3] 선택 후 다운로드

② 마더텅 홈페이지(www.toptutor.co.kr) 접속 → 상단 메뉴 중 [초등 · 유아] 의 [교재자료실] 선택
→ 자료실 상단의 [교재를 선택하세요.] 에서 해당 교재명 선택
→ 자료 목록에서 mp3 게시물 선택 후 다운로드

2. 모바일 스트리밍 / 다운로드

① 스마트폰으로 교재 뒷면의 QR코드 스캔 → MP3 스트리밍 or 다운로드

② 주소창에 m.toptutor.co.kr 또는 포털에서 '마더텅' 검색 → [MP3 자료실] 선택
→ 상단 메뉴 중 [초등 · 유아] 선택 → 해당 교재명 찾아 선택 후 MP3 스트리밍 or 다운로드

단어 쓰기 연습 1

초3800_3_w1

들려주는 단어를 잘 듣고, 세 번씩 써 보세요.

MP3 3권 단어 01

01 **speak** 동 말하다	speak		
02 **anywhere** 부 어디든	anywhere		
03 **anything** 대 무엇이든	anything		
04 **play** 동 연주하다	play		
05 **fix** 동 고치다	fix		
06 **something** 대 어떤 것	something		
07 **glass** 명 한 잔	glass		
08 **pilot** 명 조종사	pilot		
09 **seat** 명 자리	seat		
10 **sting** 동 따갑게 하다	sting		
11 **bring** 동 데려오다	bring		
12 **shoot** 동 쏘다	shoot		
13 **web** 명 거미줄	web		

들려주는 단어를 잘 듣고, 세 번씩 써 보세요.

MP3 3권 단어 01

14 **heal** ⓢ 치유되다	heal		
15 **superpower** ⓜ 초능력	superpower		
16 **suit** ⓜ 옷 (한 벌)	suit		
17 **wear** ⓢ 입다, (신발을) 신다	wear		
18 **outdoor** ⓗ 야외의	outdoor		
19 **restroom** ⓜ 화장실	restroom		
20 **cell phone** ⓜ 휴대전화	cell phone		
21 **during** ⓙ ~동안	during		
22 **leave** ⓢ 떠나다	leave		
23 **right** ⓗ 맞는	right		
24 **answer** ⓜ 답	answer		
25 **secret** ⓜ 비밀	secret		
26 **keep** ⓢ 지키다	keep		

단어 쓰기 연습 2

초3800_3_w2

들려주는 단어를 잘 듣고, 세 번씩 써 보세요.

MP3 3권 단어 02

27 **pass** ⓢ 통과하다	pass		
28 **exam** ⓜ 시험	exam		
29 **believe** ⓢ 믿다	believe		
30 **lie** ⓢ 거짓말하다	lie		
31 **pocket money** ⓜ 용돈	pocket money		
32 **order** ⓢ 주문하다	order		
33 **bite** ⓜ 한 입	bite		
34 **hurt** ⓢ 다치게 하다	hurt		
35 **game** ⓜ 시합	game		
36 **cancel** ⓢ 취소하다	cancel		
37 **change** ⓢ 바꾸다	change		
38 **life** ⓜ 삶	life		
39 **handsome** ⓗ 잘생긴	handsome		

들려주는 단어를 잘 듣고, 세 번씩 써 보세요.

MP3 3권 단어 02

40 **mean** ⓗ 못된, 심술궂은	mean		
41 **try on** ⓓ 입어 보다	try on		
42 **size** ⓜ 치수	size		
43 **right** ⓑ 즉시	right		
44 **smart** ⓗ 똑똑한	smart		
45 **story** ⓜ 이야기	story		
46 **ending** ⓜ 결말	ending		
47 **voice** ⓜ 목소리	voice		
48 **come** ⓓ (어떤 상태가) 되다	come		
49 **dream** ⓜ 꿈	dream		
50 **fresh water** ⓜ 민물	fresh water		
51 **ride** ⓓ 타다	ride		
52 **read** ⓓ 읽다	read		

단어 쓰기 연습 3

초3800_3_w3

들려주는 단어를 잘 듣고, 세 번씩 써 보세요.

MP3 3권 단어 03

01	**choose** 동 선택하다	choose			
02	**arrive** 동 도착하다	arrive			
03	**draw** 동 그리다	draw			
04	**picture** 명 그림	picture			
05	**doctor** 명 의사	doctor			
06	**sick** 형 아픈	sick			
07	**wash** 동 씻다	wash			
08	**clean** 동 청소하다	clean			
09	**get up** 동 일어나다	get up			
10	**near** 전 ~에서 가까이	near			
11	**pool** 명 수영장	pool			
12	**lie** 명 거짓말	lie			
13	**holiday** 명 휴일	holiday			

들려주는 단어를 잘 듣고, 세 번씩 써 보세요.

MP3 3권 단어 03

14 **worry** ⓢ 걱정하다	worry		
15 **warm** ⓗ 따뜻한	warm		
16 **waste** ⓢ 낭비하다	waste		
17 **bother** ⓢ 귀찮게 하다	bother		
18 **animal** ⓜ 동물	animal		
19 **drive** ⓢ 운전하다	drive		
20 **cross** ⓢ 넘다	cross		
21 **line** ⓜ 선	line		
22 **pay** ⓢ 지불하다	pay		
23 **parking** ⓜ 주차	parking		
24 **turn** ⓢ 돌다	turn		
25 **left** ⓑ 왼쪽으로	left		
26 **careful** ⓗ 조심하는	careful		

단어 쓰기 연습 4

초3800_3_w4

들려주는 단어를 잘 듣고, 세 번씩 써 보세요.

MP3 3권 단어 04

27 **zone** ⓜ 구역	zone		
28 **beach** ⓜ 해변	beach		
29 **far** ⓟ 멀리	far		
30 **sunblock** ⓜ 자외선 차단제	sunblock		
31 **put on** ⓓ 바르다	put on		
32 **textbook** ⓜ 교과서	textbook		
33 **borrow** ⓓ 빌리다	borrow		
34 **get** ⓓ 받다	get		
35 **library** ⓜ 도서관	library		
36 **wait** ⓓ 기다리다	wait		
37 **dessert** ⓜ 디저트	dessert		
38 **call** ⓓ 전화하다	call		
39 **skip** ⓓ 거르다	skip		

들려주는 단어를 잘 듣고, 세 번씩 써 보세요.

MP3 3권 단어 **04**

40 **meal** ⑲ 식사	meal		
41 **follow** ⑤ 따르다	follow		
42 **rule** ⑲ 규칙	rule		
43 **change** ⑤ 바꾸다	change		
44 **try** ⑤ 시도하다	try		
45 **forget** ⑤ 잊다	forget		
46 **power** ⑲ 힘	power		
47 **save** ⑤ 아끼다	save		
48 **plant** ⑲ 식물	plant		
49 **water** ⑤ 물을 주다	water		
50 **directly** ⑨ 직접적으로	directly		
51 **remember** ⑤ 기억하다	remember		
52 **answer sheet** ⑲ 답안지	answer sheet		

단어 쓰기 연습 5

초3800_3_w5

들려주는 단어를 잘 듣고, 세 번씩 써 보세요.

MP3 3권 단어 05

01 **beautiful** 형 아름다운	beautiful		
02 **famous** 형 유명한	famous		
03 **sour** 형 신	sour		
04 **salty** 형 짠	salty		
05 **spicy** 형 매운	spicy		
06 **bitter** 형 맛이 쓴	bitter		
07 **funny** 형 웃긴	funny		
08 **watermelon** 명 수박	watermelon		
09 **strong** 형 강한	strong		
10 **soft** 형 부드러운	soft		
11 **sweet** 형 단	sweet		
12 **cotton candy** 명 솜사탕	cotton candy		
13 **race** 명 경주	race		

들려주는 단어를 잘 듣고, 세 번씩 써 보세요.

MP3 3권 단어 05

14 **look** ⓢ ~하게 보이다	look		
15 **smell** ⓢ 냄새가 나다	smell		
16 **sound** ⓢ ~처럼 들리다	sound		
17 **taste** ⓢ 맛보다	taste		
18 **feel** ⓢ 느끼다	feel		
19 **skirt** ⓜ 치마	skirt		
20 **shy** ⓗ 수줍어하는	shy		
21 **entertainer** ⓜ 연예인	entertainer		
22 **teenager** ⓜ 10대	teenager		
23 **smart** ⓗ 똑똑한	smart		
24 **cheetah** ⓜ 치타	cheetah		
25 **tortoise** ⓜ 거북	tortoise		
26 **ant** ⓜ 개미	ant		

단어 쓰기 연습 6

초3800_3_w6

들려주는 단어를 잘 듣고, 세 번씩 써 보세요.

MP3 3권 단어 06

27 **tiny** 형 작은	tiny		
28 **humid** 형 습한	humid		
29 **same** 형 같은	same		
30 **wonderful** 형 아주 멋진	wonderful		
31 **important** 형 중요한	important		
32 **member** 명 구성원	member		
33 **full** 형 배부른	full		
34 **different** 형 다른	different		
35 **result** 명 결과	result		
36 **honest** 형 정직한	honest		
37 **favorite** 형 가장 좋아하는	favorite		
38 **ugly** 형 못생긴	ugly		
39 **strange** 형 이상한	strange		

들려주는 단어를 잘 듣고, 세 번씩 써 보세요.

MP3 3권 단어 06

40 **dirty** 형 더러운	dirty		
41 **crazy** 형 미친	crazy		
42 **special** 형 특별한	special		
43 **talent** 명 재능	talent		
44 **brave** 형 용감한	brave		
45 **alone** 형 혼자인	alone		
46 **diary** 명 일기장	diary		
47 **choice** 명 선택	choice		
48 **news** 명 소식	news		
49 **friendly** 형 친근한	friendly		
50 **difficult** 형 어려운	difficult		
51 **tired** 형 지친	tired		
52 **advice** 명 충고	advice		

단어 쓰기 연습 7

초3800_3_w7

들려주는 단어를 잘 듣고, 세 번씩 써 보세요.

MP3 3권 단어 07

01 **honestly** 부 솔직히	honestly		
02 **believe** 동 믿다	believe		
03 **sadly** 부 슬프게	sadly		
04 **newly** 부 새롭게	newly		
05 **angrily** 부 화나서	angrily		
06 **simply** 부 간단하게	simply		
07 **terribly** 부 끔찍하게	terribly		
08 **friendly** 형 친근한	friendly		
09 **lovely** 형 사랑스러운	lovely		
10 **quickly** 부 빠르게	quickly		
11 **raise** 동 들어 올리다	raise		
12 **loudly** 부 시끄럽게	loudly		
13 **softly** 부 부드럽게	softly		

들려주는 단어를 잘 듣고, 세 번씩 써 보세요.

MP3 3권 단어 07

14 **well** ㊋ 잘, 좋게	well		
15 **always** ㊋ 항상	always		
16 **usually** ㊋ 보통	usually		
17 **often** ㊋ 자주	often		
18 **sometimes** ㊋ 가끔	sometimes		
19 **seldom** ㊋ 거의 ~하지 않는	seldom		
20 **never** ㊋ 전혀 ~하지 않는	never		
21 **free** ㊎ 한가한	free		
22 **wrong** ㊎ 잘못된	wrong		
23 **borrow** ㊍ 빌리다	borrow		
24 **rice** ㊔ 쌀	rice		
25 **watch** ㊔ 시계	watch		
26 **lose** ㊍ 잃어버리다	lose		

초3800_3_w8

단어 쓰기 연습 8

들려주는 단어를 잘 듣고, 세 번씩 써 보세요.

MP3 3권 단어 08

번호	단어	뜻	쓰기		
27	lie	명 거짓말	lie		
28	again	부 다시	again		
29	climb	동 오르다	climb		
30	bamboo	명 대나무	bamboo		
31	leaf	명 잎	leaf		
32	together	부 함께	together		
33	join	동 참가하다	join		
34	festival	명 축제	festival		
35	practice	동 연습하다	practice		
36	finish	동 끝내다	finish		
37	exactly	부 정확히	exactly		
38	right	형 맞는	right		
39	heavily	부 아주 많이	heavily		

들려주는 단어를 잘 듣고, 세 번씩 써 보세요.

MP3 3권 단어 08

40 **cry** 동 울다	cry		
41 **young** 형 어린	young		
42 **still** 부 아직도	still		
43 **vacation** 명 방학	vacation		
44 **fond** 형 좋아하는	fond		
45 **sunset** 명 일몰	sunset		
46 **even** 부 ~조차	even		
47 **perfectly** 부 완벽하게	perfectly		
48 **move** 동 움직이다	move		
49 **deeply** 부 깊이	deeply		
50 **already** 부 이미	already		
51 **dangerous** 형 위험한	dangerous		
52 **movie** 명 영화	movie		

단어 쓰기 연습 9

초3800_3_w9

들려주는 단어를 잘 듣고, 세 번씩 써 보세요.

MP3 3권 단어 09

01 **kind** 형 친절한	kind		
02 **fast** 부 빨리	fast		
03 **how** 부 정말, 얼마나	how		
04 **interesting** 형 재미있는	interesting		
05 **beautiful** 형 아름다운	beautiful		
06 **star** 명 별	star		
07 **flower** 명 꽃	flower		
08 **delicious** 형 맛있는	delicious		
09 **make** 동 만들다	make		
10 **easy** 형 쉬운	easy		
11 **funny** 형 웃긴	funny		
12 **exciting** 형 흥미로운	exciting		
13 **tall** 형 (키가) 큰	tall		

들려주는 단어를 잘 듣고, 세 번씩 써 보세요.

MP3 3권 단어 09

14 **cute** ⓗ 귀여운	cute		
15 **smart** ⓗ 똑똑한	smart		
16 **look** ⓓ ~처럼 보이다	look		
17 **spring** ⓜ 봄	spring		
18 **hot** ⓗ 더운	hot		
19 **weather** ⓜ 날씨	weather		
20 **swim** ⓓ 수영하다	swim		
21 **cold** ⓗ 차가운	cold		
22 **broadly** ⓑ 활짝	broadly		
23 **smile** ⓓ 웃다	smile		
24 **elementary** ⓗ 초급의	elementary		
25 **difficult** ⓗ 어려운	difficult		
26 **question** ⓜ 문제	question		

단어 쓰기 연습 10

초3800_3_w10

들려주는 단어를 잘 듣고, 세 번씩 써 보세요.

MP3 3권 단어 10

27 **understand** ⑧ 이해하다	understand		
28 **answer** ⑧ 대답하다	answer		
29 **nice** ⑱ 친절한	nice		
30 **active** ⑱ 활동적인	active		
31 **idea** ⑲ 생각	idea		
32 **smell** ⑧ 냄새가 나다	smell		
33 **waste** ⑲ 낭비	waste		
34 **honor** ⑲ 영광	honor		
35 **clean** ⑱ 깨끗한	clean		
36 **pleasant** ⑱ 기분 좋은	pleasant		
37 **surprise** ⑲ 뜻밖의 일	surprise		
38 **voice** ⑲ 목소리	voice		
39 **lovely** ⑱ 사랑스러운	lovely		

들려주는 단어를 잘 듣고, 세 번씩 써 보세요.

MP3 3권 단어 10

40 **lazy** ⓗ 게으른	lazy		
41 **pity** ⓜ 애석한 일	pity		
42 **play** ⓓ (게임, 놀이 등을) 하다	play		
43 **hide-and-seek** ⓜ 숨바꼭질	hide-and-seek		
44 **sing** ⓓ 노래하다	sing		
45 **cover** ⓜ 표지	cover		
46 **excellent** ⓗ 훌륭한	excellent		
47 **library** ⓜ 도서관	library		
48 **large** ⓗ 큰	large		
49 **bark** ⓓ (개가) 짖다	bark		
50 **speak** ⓓ 말하다	speak		
51 **gently** ⓑ 온화하게	gently		
52 **wonderful** ⓗ 멋진	wonderful		

단어 쓰기 연습 11

초3800_3_w11

들려주는 단어를 잘 듣고, 세 번씩 써 보세요. MP3 3권 단어 11

01	**open** ⓢ (책을) 펴다	open		
02	**textbook** ⓜ 교과서	textbook		
03	**quiet** ⓗ 조용한	quiet		
04	**stand** ⓢ 일어서다	stand		
05	**afraid** ⓗ 두려워하는	afraid		
06	**crazy** ⓗ 정상이 아닌	crazy		
07	**close** ⓢ 닫다	close		
08	**bite** ⓢ 물다	bite		
09	**solve** ⓢ 풀다	solve		
10	**wait** ⓢ 기다리다	wait		
11	**mark** ⓢ 표시하다	mark		
12	**until** ⓙ ~까지	until		
13	**up** ⓑ 다 끝난	up		

들려주는 단어를 잘 듣고, 세 번씩 써 보세요.

MP3 3권 단어 11

14 **during** ㉺ ~동안에	during		
15 **boil** ㉯ 끓이다	boil		
16 **noodle** ㉱ 면	noodle		
17 **sauce** ㉱ 소스	sauce		
18 **pot** ㉱ 냄비	pot		
19 **minute** ㉱ 분	minute		
20 **picnic** ㉱ 소풍	picnic		
21 **check** ㉯ 확인하다	check		
22 **worry** ㉯ 걱정하다	worry		
23 **stranger** ㉱ 모르는 사람	stranger		
24 **matter** ㉱ 문제, 일	matter		
25 **yell** ㉯ 소리 지르다	yell		
26 **beetle** ㉱ 딱정벌레	beetle		

단어 쓰기 연습 12

초3800_3_w12

들려주는 단어를 잘 듣고, 세 번씩 써 보세요.

MP3 3권 단어 12

27 **insect** 명 곤충	insect		
28 **bring** 동 가져오다	bring		
29 **explain** 동 설명하다	explain		
30 **mistake** 명 실수	mistake		
31 **second** 형 두 번째의	second		
32 **have** 동 먹다	have		
33 **volume** 명 음량	volume		
34 **raise** 동 높이다	raise		
35 **return** 동 돌아가다	return		
36 **after** 전 후에	after		
37 **bother** 동 귀찮게 하다	bother		
38 **prepared** 형 준비가 된	prepared		
39 **truth** 명 진실	truth		

들려주는 단어를 잘 듣고, 세 번씩 써 보세요.

MP3 3권 단어 12

40 **pick** ⑧ (꽃을) 꺾다	pick		
41 **circle** ⑲ 원	circle		
42 **forget** ⑧ 잊어버리다	forget		
43 **ingredient** ⑲ 재료	ingredient		
44 **recipe** ⑲ 조리법	recipe		
45 **flour** ⑲ 밀가루	flour		
46 **bowl** ⑲ 그릇	bowl		
47 **sugar** ⑲ 설탕	sugar		
48 **mix** ⑧ 섞다	mix		
49 **kitchen** ⑲ 부엌	kitchen		
50 **fast** ⑨ 빠르게	fast		
51 **clean** ⑧ 청소하다	clean		
52 **oven** ⑲ 오븐	oven		

단어 쓰기 연습 13

초3800_3_w13

들려주는 단어를 잘 듣고, 세 번씩 써 보세요.

MP3 3권 단어 13

01 **park** ㊔ 공원	park		
02 **inside** ㊇ 안으로	inside		
03 **order** ㊂ 주문하다	order		
04 **fried** ㊒ 기름에 튀긴	fried		
05 **chicken** ㊔ 닭, 닭고기	chicken		
06 **waste** ㊂ 낭비하다	waste		
07 **have** ㊂ 가지다, 있다	have		
08 **fight** ㊂ 싸우다	fight		
09 **worry** ㊂ 걱정하다	worry		
10 **paint** ㊂ (그림을) 그리다	paint		
11 **mess** ㊂ 어지럽히다	mess		
12 **dance** ㊂ 춤추다	dance		
13 **tired** ㊒ 피곤한	tired		

들려주는 단어를 잘 듣고, 세 번씩 써 보세요.

MP3 3권 단어 13

14 **bring** ⓢ 데려오다	bring		
15 **poor** ⓗ 불쌍한	poor		
16 **wash** ⓢ 씻다	wash		
17 **bread** ⓜ 빵	bread		
18 **doctor** ⓜ 의사	doctor		
19 **travel** ⓢ 여행하다	travel		
20 **island** ⓜ 섬	island		
21 **sound** ⓢ ~인 것 같다	sound		
22 **plan** ⓜ 계획	plan		
23 **hurry** ⓢ 서두르다	hurry		
24 **enough** ⓗ 충분한	enough		
25 **need** ⓢ 필요하다	need		
26 **clothes** ⓜ 옷	clothes		

단어 쓰기 연습 14

초3800_3_w14

들려주는 단어를 잘 듣고, 세 번씩 써 보세요.

MP3 3권 단어 14

27 **busy** ⓗ 바쁜	busy		
28 **idea** ⓜ 생각	idea		
29 **horror** ⓜ 공포	horror		
30 **nightmare** ⓜ 악몽	nightmare		
31 **buy** ⓓ 사다	buy		
32 **ticket** ⓜ 표	ticket		
33 **start** ⓓ 시작하다	start		
34 **wear** ⓓ 입다	wear		
35 **skirt** ⓜ 치마	skirt		
36 **walk** ⓓ 걷다	walk		
37 **take** ⓓ 타다, (사진을) 찍다	take		
38 **leave** ⓓ ~을 두고 가다	leave		
39 **anything** ⓓ 아무것	anything		

들려주는 단어를 잘 듣고, 세 번씩 써 보세요.

MP3 3권 단어 14

40 **visit** ⓢ 방문하다	visit		
41 **present** ⓜ 선물	present		
42 **ride** ⓢ 타다	ride		
43 **check** ⓢ 확인하다	check		
44 **outside** ⓟ 밖으로	outside		
45 **river** ⓜ 강	river		
46 **different** ⓗ 다른	different		
47 **something** ⓓ 무언가	something		
48 **choose** ⓢ 정하다	choose		
49 **menu** ⓜ 메뉴	menu		
50 **Thai** ⓗ 태국의	Thai		
51 **restaurant** ⓜ 식당	restaurant		
52 **rest** ⓜ 휴식	rest		

초3800_3_d1

Dictation Test 1

MP3 3권 받아쓰기 01

Name : Date : Score : /10

[01~10] 들려주는 문장을 잘 듣고 빈칸에 알맞은 단어를 채워 보세요.

01. He __________ be a superhero.
그는 슈퍼히어로일지도 몰라.

02. I __________ swim.
난 수영할 수 있어.

03. __________ __________ like Somi.
그는 소미를 좋아할지도 몰라.

04. My little sister __________ __________ the piano.
내 여동생은 피아노를 칠 수 있어.

05. __________ __________ keep a secret?
너 비밀 지킬 수 있어?

06. __________ __________ ride a horse.
난 말을 탈 수 있어.

07. Clair __________ __________ read Korean.
Clair는 한국어를 읽지 못해.

08. You __________ watch TV.
너는 TV를 볼 수 없어.

09. This __________ __________ be the right answer.
이게 맞는 답이 아닐지도 몰라.

10. You __________ sit here.
당신은 여기 앉아도 돼요.

정답 p.238

Dictation Test 2

MP3 3권 받아쓰기 02

Name : Date : Score : /10

[01~10] 들려주는 문장을 잘 듣고 빈칸에 알맞은 단어를 채워 보세요.

01. I ____________ ____________ believe that!
난 그걸 믿을 수가 없어!

02. Jihee may ____________ ____________ the exam.
지희가 시험을 통과하지 못할지도 몰라.

03. ____________ you ____________ the dishes?
설거지 해 줄 수 있니?

04. ____________ I ____________ to the restroom?
화장실 가도 될까요?

05. ____________ ____________ snow soon.
금방 눈이 올지도 몰라.

06. I can ____________ ____________ my feet.
난 내 발을 느낄 수 없어.

07. I ____________ ____________ my life.
나는 내 삶을 바꿀 수 있다.

08. ____________ ____________ do the dishes?
설거지 해 줄 수 있니?

09. You ____________ have a seat.
자리에 앉아도 좋아요.

10. ____________ ____________ go to the restroom?
화장실 가도 될까요?

정답 p.238

초3800_3_d3

Dictation Test 3

MP3 3권 받아쓰기 **03**

Name : Date : Score : /10

[01~10] 들려주는 문장을 잘 듣고 빈칸에 알맞은 단어를 채워 보세요.

01. You ________ ________ drive a car.
당신은 운전하면 안 됩니다.

02. We ________ have to order a dessert.
우리는 디저트를 주문하지 않아도 돼.

03. You ________ ________ turn left here.
여기서 좌회전하시면 안 됩니다.

04. We ________ have to pay.
우리는 돈을 내지 않아도 돼.

05. You ________ ________ swim far.
넌 멀리 수영하면 안 된다.

06. ________ ________ read the textbooks.
넌 교과서를 읽어야 해.

07. Jisun ________ ________ for the math exam.
지선이는 수학 시험을 위해 공부해야 한다.

08. Minji ________ ________ borrow my notes.
민지는 내 노트를 빌려야 했어.

09. You ________ ________ ________ get a B.
너는 B를 받아야 할 것이다

10. ________ ________ go to the library.
난 도서관에 가야 해.

정답 p.238

초3800_3_d4

Dictation Test 4

MP3 3권 받아쓰기 04

Name : Date : Score : /10

[01~10] 들려주는 문장을 잘 듣고 빈칸에 알맞은 단어를 채워 보세요.

01. ________ ________ wait for the dinner.
우리는 저녁식사를 기다려야 해.

02. I have to ________.
난 기억해야만 해.

03. You ________ ________ here.
여러분은 여기에서 멈춰야 합니다.

04. ________ I ________ ________ wear pants?
저 바지 입어야 해요?

05. ________ I have to ________ dinner?
저 저녁 먹어야 해요?

06. She ________ ________ drink milk.
그녀는 우유를 마셔야 합니다.

07. You ________ ________ ________ worry.
너는 걱정할 필요 없어.

08. ________ have to ________ my mom.
나 엄마한테 전화해야 해.

09. You must ________ ________ this line.
이 선을 넘으면 안 됩니다.

10. He ________ ________ change his clothes.
그는 옷을 갈아입어야만 해.

정답 p.238

초3800_3_d5

Dictation Test 5

MP3 3권 받아쓰기 05

Name : Date : Score : /10

[01~10] 들려주는 문장을 잘 듣고 빈칸에 알맞은 단어를 채워 보세요.

01. She is ______________.

그녀는 예뻐.

02. My dog is ______________.

나의 개는 영리해.

03. Do you like ______________ candy?

넌 달콤한 사탕을 좋아해?

04. It is ______________ today.

오늘 비 와.

05. I don't like a ______________ day.

나는 바람 많이 부는 날을 좋아하지 않아.

06. Sihu is very ______________.

시후는 아주 친절하다.

07. Sunday is my ______________ day.

일요일은 내가 가장 좋아하는 날이야.

08. I don't have ______________ talents.

나는 특별한 재능을 가지고 있지 않다.

09. Today is a ______________ ______________.

오늘은 힘든 날이야.

10. The English test is ______________.

영어 시험은 어려워.

정답 p.238

초3800_3_d6

Dictation Test 6

MP3 3권 받아쓰기 **06**

Name : Date : Score : /10

[01~10] 들려주는 문장을 잘 듣고 빈칸에 알맞은 단어를 채워 보세요.

01. We ________________ ________________.

우리는 준비가 됐어.

02. I ________________ ________________.

나 배불러.

03. The park is ________________.

그 공원은 아름다워.

04. Why are your hands ________________?

왜 당신의 손은 지저분해요?

05. It is too ________________ today.

오늘 너무 덥다.

06. I am not ________________.

나는 미치지 않았어.

07. He is ________________ and ________________.

그는 크고 못생겼어.

08. The dog has ________________ legs.

그 개는 다리가 짧아.

09. Jane has a ________________ voice.

Jane은 좋은 목소리를 갖고 있다.

10. I want a ________________ ________________.

나는 맛있는 케이크를 원해.

정답 p.238

초3800_3_d7

Dictation Test 7

MP3 3권 받아쓰기 07

Name : Date : Score : /10

[01~10] 들려주는 문장을 잘 듣고 빈칸에 알맞은 단어를 채워 보세요.

01. A lion walks ______________.
사자는 느리게 걸어.

02. She plays the music ______________.
그녀는 음악을 크게 틀어.

03. I ______________ go to the zoo.
나는 동물원에 자주 가.

04. She runs ______________ to school.
그녀는 학교로 빨리 뛰어가.

05. ______________, I can't believe it.
솔직히, 나는 그것을 믿을 수 없어요.

06. It's ______________ dangerous.
그것은 너무 위험하다.

07. Our English teacher is ______________ ______________.
우리 영어 선생님은 매우 친절하셔.

08. When can we meet ______________?
우리 언제 또 만날 수 있지?

09. Monkeys climb trees ______________.
원숭이들은 나무를 잘 타.

10. Bora and Junwoo dance ______________.
보라와 준우는 함께 춤춰.

정답 p.238

초3800_3_d8

Dictation Test 8

MP3 3권 받아쓰기 08

Name : Date : Score : /10

[01~10] 들려주는 문장을 잘 듣고 빈칸에 알맞은 단어를 채워 보세요.

01. That's ________________ right.

그것은 정확히 맞아.

02. He looks ________________ ________________.

그는 매우 멋져 보여.

03. He is ________________ in the hospital.

그는 아직도 병원에 있다.

04. He wakes up ________________.

그는 늦게 일어난다.

05. It is ________________ 11:00 p.m.

벌써 밤 11시야.

06. I ________________ ________________ movies.

난 정말 영화를 좋아해.

07. I sleep ________________.

나는 잠을 깊이 잔다.

08. Mina ________________ takes piano lessons.

미나는 항상 피아노 수업을 들어.

09. She ________________ eats chocolate.

그녀는 초콜릿을 거의 먹지 않아.

10. He is ________________ ________________.

그는 너무 어려.

정답 p.238

초3800_3_d9

Dictation Test 9

MP3 3권 받아쓰기 09

Name : Date : Score : /10

[01~10] 들려주는 문장을 잘 듣고 빈칸에 알맞은 단어를 채워 보세요.

01. ________________ warm it is!

정말 따뜻하구나!

02. ________________ a wonderful spring!

아주 멋진 봄이구나!

03. How ________________ she is!

그녀는 아주 친절하구나!

04. What a ________________ ________________!

참 좋은 친구다!

05. How ________________ she swims!

그녀는 수영을 정말 잘하는구나!

06. How ________________!

정말 깨끗하구나!

07. What ________________ ________________!

아주 영광스럽구나!

08. How fast ________________ ________________!

그는 참 빠르게 달리는구나!

09. ________________ ________________ the dog is!

그 개는 정말 게으르구나!

10. What a fast train ________________ ________________ !

그것은 정말 빠른 기차구나!

정답 p.238

초3800_3_d10

Dictation Test 10

MP3 3권 받아쓰기 10

Name : Date : Score : /10

[01~10] 들려주는 문장을 잘 듣고 빈칸에 알맞은 단어를 채워 보세요.

01. ________________ well you draw!

너는 참 그림을 잘 그리는구나!

02. What a ________________ ________________!

아주 좋은 생각이구나!

03. ________________ an active girl!

아주 활동적인 소녀구나!

04. How ________________ his feet are!

그의 발은 정말 작구나!

05. How ________________ it is!

정말 어둡구나!

06. What a wonderful ________________!

정말 멋진 누나구나!

07. What ________________ ________________ it is!

날씨가 참 덥구나!

08. ________________ ________________ the dinner smells!

저녁 식사 냄새가 참 좋구나!

09. ________________ ________________ lovely voice!

정말 사랑스러운 목소리구나!

10. What a ________________!

참 애석한 일이구나!

정답 p.238

초3800_3_d11

Dictation Test 11

MP3 3권 받아쓰기 11

Name : Date : Score : /10

[01~10] 들려주는 문장을 잘 듣고 빈칸에 알맞은 단어를 채워 보세요.

01. ________________ here!
이리로 와봐!

02. ________________ water.
물을 끓이세요.

03. Ok, ________________ ________________ the car.
그래, 차에 타렴.

04. ________________ your books ________________.
여러분의 책들을 치우세요.

05. ________________ ________________ because it is hot.
뜨거우니까 조심하세요.

06. ________________ be afraid of mistakes.
실수를 두려워하지 마세요.

07. ________________ a break.
쉬세요.

08. Be quiet and ________________.
조용히 하고 들어보세요.

09. ________________ bother me.
나를 귀찮게 하지 마.

10. ________________ ________________ the truth.
나에게 진실을 말해줘.

정답 p.238

초3800_3_d12

Dictation Test 12

MP3 3권 받아쓰기 12

Name : Date : Score : /10

[01~10] 들려주는 문장을 잘 듣고 빈칸에 알맞은 단어를 채워 보세요.

01. Don't ________________ your homework.
숙제 잊지 마.

02. Finally, ________________ the kitchen.
마지막으로, 부엌을 청소해.

03. ________________ for 10 minutes.
10분 기다려.

04. Don't ________________ fast.
빠르게 말하지 마.

05. ________________ ________________ a supermarket tomorrow.
내일 슈퍼마켓에 가.

06. ________________ some chocolate.
초콜릿 좀 먹어.

07. ________________ your math textbooks.
수학 교과서 펴세요.

08. ________________ the questions.
문제를 푸세요.

09. ________________ ________________, Mom. I have everything.
걱정하지 마세요, 엄마. 다 있어요.

10. Raise the ________________.
음량을 높여줘.

정답 p.238

초3800_3_d13

Dictation Test 13

MP3 3권 받아쓰기 13

Name : Date : Score : /10

[01~10] 들려주는 문장을 잘 듣고 빈칸에 알맞은 단어를 채워 보세요.

01. ________________ make a plan.

계획을 짜보자.

02. Let's ________________ hurry.

서두르지 말자.

03. ________________ ________________ ________________ take a break?

잠깐 쉬는 게 어때?

04. Why don't you ________________ home?

걸어서 집에 가는 건 어때?

05. ________________ ________________ wear this red skirt?

이 빨간 치마를 입는 건 어때?

06. Why not ________________ a picture?

사진을 한 장 찍는 건 어떨까?

07. Let's ________________ a bike.

자전거를 타자.

08. ________________ ________________ going to the Han River?

한강 가는 거 어때?

09. Why not ________________ ________________ a picnic?

소풍 가는 건 어때?

10. Let's not ________________ our plan.

우리의 계획을 잊지 말자.

정답 p.238

초3800_3_d14

Dictation Test 14

MP3 3권 받아쓰기 14

Name : Date : Score : /10

[01~10] 들려주는 문장을 잘 듣고 빈칸에 알맞은 단어를 채워 보세요.

01. Why not ________ ________?

나가서 먹을까?

02. Let's ________ ________ outside.

밖에 나가지 말자.

03. How about ________ soccer at the park?

공원에서 축구를 하는 건 어때?

04. ________ ________ ________ clean your room?

네 방을 좀 치우는 건 어때?

05. ________ visit a museum.

박물관에 가자.

06. ________ ________ watch a movie?

영화를 보는 건 어때?

07. ________ ________ watching "The Jungle Book"?

'정글북'을 보는 건 어때?

08. Why don't you ________ with us?

우리랑 같이 있는 건 어때?

09. Why don't you ________ some pizza?

피자를 좀 주문하는 건 어때?

10. ________ ________ be late.

늦지 말자.

정답 p.238

단어테스트 1

다음 한글 뜻을 보고 영어 표현을 적으세요. Name : Date : Score : /26

01		동 말하다	14		동 치유되다
02		부 어디든	15		명 초능력
03		대 무엇이든	16		명 옷 (한 벌)
04		동 연주하다	17		동 입다, (신발을) 신다
05		동 고치다	18		형 야외의
06		대 어떤 것	19		명 화장실
07		명 한 잔	20		명 휴대전화
08		명 조종사	21		전 ~동안
09		명 자리	22		동 떠나다
10		동 따갑게 하다	23		형 맞는
11		동 데려오다	24		명 답
12		동 쏘다	25		명 비밀
13		명 거미줄	26		동 지키다

정답 p.238

단어테스트 2

다음 한글 뜻을 보고 영어 표현을 적으세요. Name : Date : Score : /26

01		동 통과하다	14		형 못된, 심술궂은
02		명 시험	15		동 입어 보다
03		동 믿다	16		명 치수
04		동 거짓말하다	17		부 즉시
05		명 용돈	18		형 똑똑한
06		동 주문하다	19		명 이야기
07		명 한 입	20		명 결말
08		동 다치게 하다	21		명 목소리
09		명 시합	22		동 (어떤 상태가) 되다
10		동 취소하다	23		명 꿈
11		동 바꾸다	24		명 민물
12		명 삶	25		동 타다
13		형 잘생긴	26		동 읽다

정답 p.238

단어테스트 3

다음 한글 뜻을 보고 영어 표현을 적으세요. Name : Date : Score : /26

01		동 선택하다	14		동 걱정하다
02		동 도착하다	15		형 따뜻한
03		동 그리다	16		동 낭비하다
04		명 그림	17		동 귀찮게 하다
05		명 의사	18		명 동물
06		형 아픈	19		동 운전하다
07		동 씻다	20		동 넘다
08		동 청소하다	21		명 선
09		동 일어나다	22		동 지불하다
10		전 ~에서 가까이	23		명 주차
11		명 수영장	24		동 돌다
12		명 거짓말	25		부 왼쪽으로
13		명 휴일	26		형 조심하는

정답 p.238

단어테스트 4

다음 한글 뜻을 보고 영어 표현을 적으세요. Name : Date : Score : /26

01		명 구역	14		명 식사
02		명 해변	15		동 따르다
03		부 멀리	16		명 규칙
04		명 자외선 차단제	17		동 바꾸다
05		동 바르다	18		동 시도하다
06		명 교과서	19		동 잊다
07		동 빌리다	20		명 힘
08		동 받다	21		동 아끼다
09		명 도서관	22		명 식물
10		동 기다리다	23		동 물을 주다
11		명 디저트	24		부 직접적으로
12		동 전화하다	25		동 기억하다
13		동 거르다	26		명 답안지

정답 p. 238

단어테스트 5

다음 한글 뜻을 보고 영어 표현을 적으세요. Name : Date : Score : /26

번호	답	뜻	번호	답	뜻
01		형 아름다운	14		동 ~하게 보이다
02		형 유명한	15		동 냄새가 나다
03		형 신	16		동 ~처럼 들리다
04		형 짠	17		동 맛보다
05		형 매운	18		동 느끼다
06		형 맛이 쓴	19		명 치마
07		형 웃긴	20		형 수줍어하는
08		명 수박	21		명 연예인
09		형 강한	22		명 10대
10		형 부드러운	23		형 똑똑한
11		형 단	24		명 치타
12		명 솜사탕	25		명 거북
13		명 경주	26		명 개미

정답 p.239

단어테스트 6

다음 한글 뜻을 보고 영어 표현을 적으세요. Name : Date : Score : /26

01		형 작은	14		형 더러운
02		형 습한	15		형 미친
03		형 같은	16		형 특별한
04		형 아주 멋진	17		명 재능
05		형 중요한	18		형 용감한
06		명 구성원	19		형 혼자인
07		형 배부른	20		명 일기장
08		형 다른	21		명 선택
09		명 결과	22		명 소식
10		형 정직한	23		형 친근한
11		형 가장 좋아하는	24		형 어려운
12		형 못생긴	25		형 지친
13		형 이상한	26		명 충고

정답 p.239

단어테스트 7

다음 한글 뜻을 보고 영어 표현을 적으세요. Name : Date : Score : /26

01 ㊕ 솔직히
02 ㊐ 믿다
03 ㊕ 슬프게
04 ㊕ 새롭게
05 ㊕ 화나서
06 ㊕ 간단하게
07 ㊕ 끔찍하게
08 ㊓ 친근한
09 ㊓ 사랑스러운
10 ㊕ 빠르게
11 ㊐ 들어 올리다
12 ㊕ 시끄럽게
13 ㊕ 부드럽게
14 ㊕ 잘, 좋게
15 ㊕ 항상
16 ㊕ 보통
17 ㊕ 자주
18 ㊕ 가끔
19 ㊕ 거의 ~하지 않는
20 ㊕ 전혀 ~하지 않는
21 ㊓ 한가한
22 ㊓ 잘못된
23 ㊐ 빌리다
24 ㊔ 쌀
25 ㊔ 시계
26 ㊐ 잃어버리다

정답 p.239

단어테스트 8

다음 한글 뜻을 보고 영어 표현을 적으세요. Name : Date : Score : /26

01	ⓜ 거짓말	14	ⓓ 울다
02	ⓑ 다시	15	ⓗ 어린
03	ⓓ 오르다	16	ⓑ 아직도
04	ⓜ 대나무	17	ⓜ 방학
05	ⓜ 잎	18	ⓗ 좋아하는
06	ⓑ 함께	19	ⓜ 일몰
07	ⓓ 참가하다	20	ⓑ ~조차
08	ⓜ 축제	21	ⓑ 완벽하게
09	ⓓ 연습하다	22	ⓓ 움직이다
10	ⓓ 끝내다	23	ⓑ 깊이
11	ⓑ 정확히	24	ⓑ 이미
12	ⓗ 맞는	25	ⓗ 위험한
13	ⓑ 아주 많이	26	ⓜ 영화

정답 p.239

단어테스트 9

다음 한글 뜻을 보고 영어 표현을 적으세요. Name : Date : Score : /26

01			형 친절한
02			부 빨리
03			부 정말, 얼마나
04			형 재미있는
05			형 아름다운
06			명 별
07			명 꽃
08			형 맛있는
09			동 만들다
10			형 쉬운
11			형 웃긴
12			형 흥미로운
13			형 (키가) 큰
14			형 귀여운
15			형 똑똑한
16			동 ~처럼 보이다
17			명 봄
18			형 더운
19			명 날씨
20			동 수영하다
21			형 차가운
22			부 활짝
23			동 웃다
24			형 초급의
25			형 어려운
26			명 문제

정답 p.239

단어테스트 10

다음 한글 뜻을 보고 영어 표현을 적으세요. Name : Date : Score : /26

01		동 이해하다	14		형 게으른
02		동 대답하다	15		명 애석한 일
03		형 친절한	16		동 (게임, 놀이 등을) 하다
04		형 활동적인	17		명 숨바꼭질
05		명 생각	18		동 노래하다
06		동 냄새가 나다	19		명 표지
07		명 낭비	20		형 훌륭한
08		명 영광	21		명 도서관
09		형 깨끗한	22		형 큰
10		형 기분 좋은	23		동 (개가) 짖다
11		명 뜻밖의 일	24		동 말하다
12		명 목소리	25		부 온화하게
13		형 사랑스러운	26		형 멋진

정답 p.239

단어테스트 11

다음 한글 뜻을 보고 영어 표현을 적으세요. Name : Date : Score : /26

01		동 (책을) 펴다	
02		명 교과서	
03		형 조용한	
04		동 일어서다	
05		형 무서운	
06		형 정상이 아닌	
07		동 닫다	
08		동 물다	
09		동 풀다	
10		동 기다리다	
11		동 표시하다	
12		전 ~까지	
13		부 다 끝난	
14		전 ~동안에	
15		동 끓이다	
16		명 면	
17		명 소스	
18		명 냄비	
19		명 분	
20		명 소풍	
21		동 확인하다	
22		동 걱정하다	
23		명 모르는 사람	
24		명 문제, 일	
25		동 소리 지르다	
26		명 딱정벌레	

정답 p.239

단어테스트 12

다음 한글 뜻을 보고 영어 표현을 적으세요. Name : Date : Score : /26

01		명 곤충	14		동 (꽃을) 꺾다
02		동 가져오다	15		명 원
03		동 설명하다	16		동 잊어버리다
04		명 실수	17		명 재료
05		형 두 번째의	18		명 조리법
06		동 먹다	19		명 밀가루
07		명 음량	20		명 그릇
08		동 높이다	21		명 설탕
09		동 돌아가다	22		동 섞다
10		전 후에	23		명 부엌
11		동 귀찮게 하다	24		부 빠르게
12		형 준비가 된	25		동 청소하다
13		명 진실	26		명 오븐

정답 p.239

단어테스트 13

다음 한글 뜻을 보고 영어 표현을 적으세요. Name : Date : Score : /26

01		명 공원	14		동 데려오다
02		부 안으로	15		형 불쌍한
03		동 주문하다	16		동 씻다
04		형 기름에 튀긴	17		명 빵
05		명 닭, 닭고기	18		명 의사
06		동 낭비하다	19		동 여행하다
07		동 가지다, 있다	20		명 섬
08		동 싸우다	21		동 ~인 것 같다
09		동 걱정하다	22		명 계획
10		동 (그림을) 그리다	23		동 서두르다
11		동 어지럽히다	24		형 충분한
12		동 춤추다	25		동 필요하다
13		형 피곤한	26		명 옷

정답 p.239

단어테스트 14

다음 한글 뜻을 보고 영어 표현을 적으세요. Name : Date : Score : /26

01		형 바쁜	14		동 방문하다
02		명 생각	15		명 선물
03		명 공포	16		동 타다
04		명 악몽	17		동 확인하다
05		동 사다	18		부 밖으로
06		명 표	19		명 강
07		동 시작하다	20		형 다른
08		동 입다	21		대 무언가
09		명 치마	22		동 정하다
10		동 걷다	23		명 메뉴
11		동 타다, (사진을) 찍다	24		형 태국의
12		동 ~을 두고 가다	25		명 식당
13		대 아무것	26		명 휴식

정답 p.239

워크북 정답

Dictation Test 1

01. may
02. can
03. He, may
04. can, play
05. Can, you
06. I, can
07. can, not
08. can't
09. may, not
10. may

Dictation Test 2

01. can, not
02. not, pass
03. Can, do
04. May, go
05. It, may
06. not, feel
07. can, change
08. Can, you
09. may
10. May, I

Dictation Test 3

01. must, not
02. don't
03. must, not
04. don't
05. must, not
06. You, must
07. must, study
08. had, to
09. will, have, to
10. I, must

Dictation Test 4

01. We, must
02. remember
03. must, stop
04. Do, have, to
05. Do, eat
06. has, to
07. don't, have, to
08. I, call
09. not, cross
10. has, to

Dictation Test 5

01. pretty
02. smart
03. sweet
04. rainy
05. windy
06. kind
07. favorite
08. special
09. hard, day
10. difficult

Dictation Test 6

01. are, ready
02. am, full
03. beautiful
04. dirty
05. hot
06. crazy
07. big, ugly
08. short
09. good
10. yummy, cake

Dictation Test 7

01. slowly
02. loudly
03. often
04. fast
05. Honestly
06. too
07. very, kind
08. again
09. well
10. together

Dictation Test 8

01. exactly
02. very, nice
03. still
04. late
05. already
06. really, like
07. deeply
08. always
09. seldom
10. too, young

Dictation Test 9

01. How
02. What
03. kind
04. good, friend
05. well
06. clean
07. an, honor
08. he, runs
09. How, lazy
10. it, is

Dictation Test 10

01. How
02. good, idea
03. What
04. small
05. dark
06. sister
07. hot, weather
08. How, great
09. What, a
10. pity

Dictation Test 11

01. Come
02. Boil
03. get, in
04. Put, away
05. Be, careful
06. Don't
07. Take
08. listen
09. Don't
10. Tell, me

Dictation Test 12

01. forget
02. clean
03. Wait
04. talk
05. Go, to
06. Have
07. Open
08. Solve
09. Don't, worry
10. volume

Dictation Test 13

01. Let's
02. not
03. Why, don't, you
04. walk
05. Why, not
06. take
07. ride
08. How, about
09. go, on
10. forget

Dictation Test 14

01. eat, out
02. not, go
03. playing
04. Why, don't, you
05. Let's
06. Why, not
07. How, about
08. stay
09. order
10. Let's, not

단어테스트 1

01. speak
02. anywhere
03. anything
04. play
05. fix
06. something
07. glass
08. pilot
09. seat
10. sting
11. bring
12. shoot
13. web
14. heal
15. superpower
16. suit
17. wear
18. outdoor
19. restroom
20. cell phone
21. during
22. leave
23. right
24. answer
25. secret
26. keep

단어테스트 2

01. pass
02. exam
03. believe
04. lie
05. pocket money
06. order
07. bite
08. hurt
09. game
10. cancel
11. change
12. life
13. handsome
14. mean
15. try on
16. size
17. right
18. smart
19. story
20. ending
21. voice
22. come
23. dream
24. fresh water
25. ride
26. read

단어테스트 3

01. choose
02. arrive
03. draw
04. picture
05. doctor
06. sick
07. wash
08. clean
09. get up
10. near
11. pool
12. lie
13. holiday
14. worry
15. warm
16. waste
17. bother
18. animal
19. drive
20. cross
21. line
22. pay
23. parking
24. turn
25. left
26. careful

단어테스트 4

01. zone
02. beach
03. far
04. sunblock
05. put on
06. textbook

07. borrow
08. get
09. library
10. wait
11. dessert
12. call
13. skip
14. meal
15. follow
16. rule
17. change
18. try
19. forget
20. power
21. save
22. plant
23. water
24. directly
25. remember
26. answer sheet

단어테스트 5

01. beautiful
02. famous
03. sour
04. salty
05. spicy
06. bitter
07. funny
08. watermelon
09. strong
10. soft
11. sweet
12. cotton candy
13. race
14. look
15. smell
16. sound
17. taste
18. feel
19. skirt
20. shy
21. entertainer
22. teenager
23. smart
24. cheetah
25. tortoise
26. ant

단어테스트 6

01. tiny
02. humid
03. same
04. wonderful
05. important
06. member

07. full
08. different
09. result
10. honest
11. favorite
12. ugly
13. strange
14. dirty
15. crazy
16. special
17. talent
18. brave
19. alone
20. diary
21. choice
22. news
23. friendly
24. difficult
25. tired
26. advice

단어테스트 7

01. honestly
02. believe
03. sadly
04. newly
05. angrily
06. simply
07. terribly
08. friendly
09. lovely
10. quickly
11. raise
12. loudly
13. softly
14. well
15. always
16. usually
17. often
18. sometimes
19. seldom
20. never
21. free
22. wrong
23. borrow
24. rice
25. watch
26. lose

단어테스트 8

01. lie
02. again
03. climb
04. bamboo
05. leaf
06. together

07. join
08. festival
09. practice
10. finish
11. exactly
12. right
13. heavily
14. cry
15. young
16. still
17. vacation
18. fond
19. sunset
20. even
21. perfectly
22. move
23. deeply
24. already
25. dangerous
26. movie

단어테스트 9

01. kind
02. fast
03. how
04. interesting
05. beautiful
06. star
07. flower
08. delicious
09. make
10. easy
11. funny
12. exciting
13. tall
14. cute
15. smart
16. look
17. spring
18. hot
19. weather
20. swim
21. cold
22. broadly
23. smile
24. elementary
25. difficult
26. question

단어테스트 10

01. understand
02. answer
03. nice
04. active
05. idea
06. smell

07. waste
08. honor
09. clean
10. pleasant
11. surprise
12. voice
13. lovely
14. lazy
15. pity
16. play
17. hide-and-seek
18. sing
19. cover
20. excellent
21. library
22. large
23. bark
24. speak
25. gently
26. wonderful

단어테스트 11

01. open
02. textbook
03. quiet
04. stand
05. afraid
06. crazy
07. close
08. bite
09. solve
10. wait
11. mark
12. until
13. up
14. during
15. boil
16. noodle
17. sauce
18. pot
19. minute
20. picnic
21. check
22. worry
23. stranger
24. matter
25. yell
26. beetle

단어테스트 12

01. insect
02. bring
03. explain
04. mistake
05. second
06. have

07. volume
08. raise
09. return
10. after
11. bother
12. prepared
13. truth
14. pick
15. circle
16. forget
17. ingredient
18. recipe
19. flour
20. bowl
21. sugar
22. mix
23. kitchen
24. fast
25. clean
26. oven

단어테스트 13

01. park
02. inside
03. order
04. fried
05. chicken
06. waste
07. have
08. fight
09. worry
10. paint
11. mess
12. dance
13. tired
14. bring
15. poor
16. wash
17. bread
18. doctor
19. travel
20. island
21. sound
22. plan
23. hurry
24. enough
25. need
26. clothes

단어테스트 14

01. busy
02. idea
03. horror
04. nightmare
05. buy
06. ticket

07. start
08. wear
09. skirt
10. walk
11. take
12. leave
13. anything
14. visit
15. present
16. ride
17. check
18. outside
19. river
20. different
21. something
22. choose
23. menu
24. Thai
25. restaurant
26. rest

정답은 뒷면에서 확인하세요.

Choose and write.

알맞은 것을 보기에서 골라 쓰세요.

보기 **ip** **it** **ix**

1.

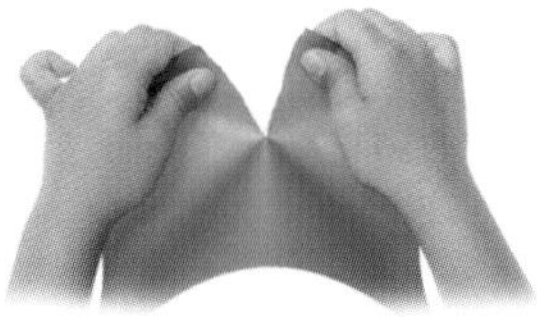

rip

2.

m___

3.

h___

4.

z___

5.

s___

6.

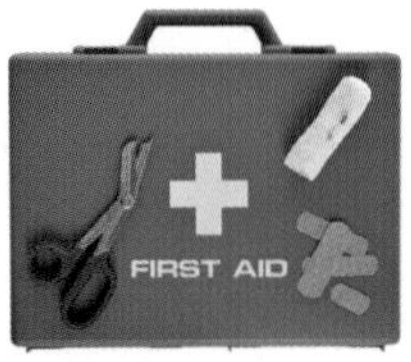

k___

Choose and write.

알맞은 것을 보기에서 골라 쓰세요.

보기 **ip** **it** **ix**

1.

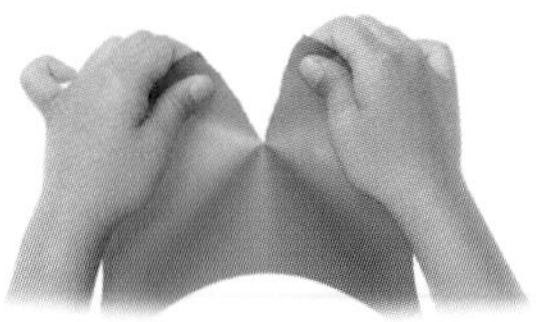

rip

2.

mix

3.

hit

4.

zip

5.

six

6.

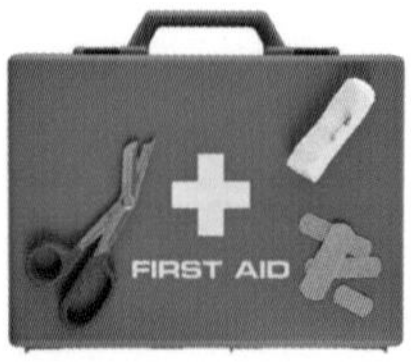

kit

MOTHERTONGUE
마더텅출판사
since1999.4.1.

초등영문법 3800제

정답과 해설

LEVEL 3

기초1단계 조동사 / 형용사 / 부사 / 감탄문 / 명령문 / 청유문

영문법 판매 1위,
초등 시리즈 초등영문법 3800제 동영상 강의

초등영문법에 필요한 것만 모았습니다.
영어에 대한 고민이 있으시면 저희 마더텅과 함께 하면 달라집니다.

마더텅과 함께하는 단계별 레벨업 강의
1단계부터 8단계까지 단계별 체계적인 영문법 학습

친절한 Q&A 게시판
친절하고 자세한 Q&A 게시판에서 강의를 수강하다 생긴 모든 궁금증을 해결

오현진 선생님

초등영문법 3800제 level 1~4

어려운 영어를 쉬운 설명으로 쉽게 가보자!

- 현 마더텅 고등영어 강사
- 현 대치동 새움학원 대표고등강사
- 현 강남구청 인터넷 수능 방송 강사
- 현 수박씨닷컴 중등영어 대표강사 [수강생 강의만족도 100%]

최주영 선생님

초등영문법 3800제 level 5~8

영어, 고민하지 마시고 꽃길만 걷게 해드립니다!

- 현 마더텅 고등영어 강사
- 현 대치동 위자듀 재수종합 독해 강사
- 현 전국 중고등학교 입시진로 강사
- 전 글로벌 1st 고등 영어 전임 강사

강의 구성

※ 강의 수, 가격 등은 당사 사정에 따라 변경될 수 있습니다.

교재명	가격	강의 수	수강 기간
초등영문법 3800제 LEVEL 1	5,900원	30강	150일(무료 수강연장 1회)
초등영문법 3800제 LEVEL 2	5,900원	26강	150일(무료 수강연장 1회)
초등영문법 3800제 LEVEL 3	5,900원	30강	150일(무료 수강연장 1회)
초등영문법 3800제 LEVEL 4	5,900원	34강	150일(무료 수강연장 1회)
초등영문법 3800제 LEVEL 5	5,900원	22강	150일(무료 수강연장 1회)
초등영문법 3800제 LEVEL 6	5,900원	23강	150일(무료 수강연장 1회)
초등영문법 3800제 LEVEL 7	5,900원	22강	150일(무료 수강연장 1회)
초등영문법 3800제 LEVEL 8	5,900원	20강	150일(무료 수강연장 1회)
초등영문법 3800제 LEVEL 1~8	39,900원	207강	365일(무료 수강연장 1회)

초등영문법 3800제

정답과 해설

LEVEL 3

기초1단계

Chapter 01 조동사

Unit 01 조동사 can

Check and Write
▶ 본문 p.9

2. do 3. be 4. can 5. Can

Unit 02 조동사 may

Check and Write
▶ 본문 p.11

2. may 3. may not 4. May
5. may not

Practice 1
▶ 본문 p.12

A 2. can 3. cannot 4. can 5. cannot
B 1. cannot[may not] 2. May 3. may
4. cannot[may not] 5. may
6. may not
C 1. Can 2. can 3. may not 4. cannot
D 1. Can 2. can't 3. can
4. may not 5. may

Practice 2
▶ 본문 p.14

2. can play the piano
3. I can swim
난 수영할 수 있어.
4. may not come to school
5. he can't play the game
6. It may rain
7. the soccer game may be cancelled
8. I can change my life
나는 내 삶을 바꿀 수 있다.
9. I may play video games
10. He may be handsome
11. May I try on
12. we can order it
13. He may not be smart
14. He may like Somi
그는 소미를 좋아할지도 몰라.
15. I can't believe it
난 그것을 믿을 수 없어.
16. Can I speak
17. I can help you
난 너를 도와줄 수 있어.
18. Your story may not have
19. Your voice can change the world
여러분의 목소리가(의견이) 세상을 바꿀 수 있습니다.
20. Our dreams can come true
우리의 꿈들은 실현될 수 있다.

Practice 3
▶ 본문 p.17

2. Some sharks can live
3. Can you ride a bicycle
너 자전거 탈 수 있어?
4. Clair cannot[can't] read Korean
Clair는 한국어를 읽지 못해.
5. She can understand
6. Can she understand English
그녀는 영어를 이해할 수 있니?
7. May[Can] I take a picture
제가 사진을 찍어도 될까요?
8. I cannot[can't] type Korean
9. Usain Bolt can run
10. You may[can] use
11. You may[can] go to the bathroom
넌 화장실에 가도 좋아.
12. You may[can] sit here
당신은 여기 앉아도 돼요.
13. LG may[can] win
14. LG can't[cannot] beat Doosan
15. It may snow
16. I cannot[can't] feel
17. You may[can] stay at our house
넌 우리 집에 있어도 좋아.
18. You cannot[can't/may not] watch TV
너는 TV를 볼 수 없어.
19. I cannot[can't] use the computer
나는 컴퓨터를 사용할 수 없어.

Let's Practice More!

SET 01
▶ 본문 p.19

02. heal 03. pass 04. order
05. play 06. rain 07. like
08. change 09. understand 10. run
11. win 12. snow

SET 02
▶ 본문 p.20

02. O 03. have 04. O 05. leave
06. O 07. eat 08. swim 09. O
10. rain 11. be 12. O 13. be
14. O

SET 03
▶ 본문 p.21

02. can live 03. cannot read
04. can understand 05. can't type 06. can run
07. may sit 08. can't beat 09. may stay
10. cannot use 11. may have 12. may not
13. may order 14. can eat

SET 04
▶ 본문 p.22

02. 허 03. 능 04. 허 05. 능
06. 허 07. 능 08. 허 09. 허
10. 능 11. 허 12. 능

SET 05
▶ 본문 p.23

02. 추 03. 추 04. 허 05. 추
06. 허 07. 허 08. 추 09. 추
10. 허 11. 추 12. 추 13. 허
14. 추

SET 06

▶ 본문 p.24

02. can 03. can't 04. may, not 05. can
06. can 07. can't 08. can't 09. can
10. can 11. can 12. may, not
13. may, not 14. can

SET 07

▶ 본문 p.26

02. cannot[can't], believe 03. cannot[can't], fly
04. cannot[can't], wear 05. may, not, be
06. can, tell 07. may, not, give
08. may, not, come 09. cannot[can't], type
10. cannot[can't], feel 11. cannot[can't], watch
12. cannot[can't], use 13. can, tell
14. may, be 15. can, order
16. can, help 17. may, not, have
18. can, ride 19. can, live
20. cannot[can't], beat

SET 08

▶ 본문 p.28

02. I cannot[can't] believe that
나는 그것을 믿을 수가 없어!

03. Mom may not give me pocket money
엄마가 나에게 용돈을 안 주실지도 몰라.

04. Can you swim
너는 수영할 수 있니?

05. Can't he play the game with us
그는 우리와 함께 경기를 할 수 없니?

06. The soccer game may not be cancelled
그 축구 시합이 취소되지 않을지도 몰라.

07. Can I change my life
내가 내 삶을 바꿀 수 있을까?

08. He cannot[can't] ride a bicycle
그는 자전거를 탈 수 없어.

09. Clair cannot[can't] read Korean
Clair는 한국어를 읽지 못해.

10. Can she understand English
그녀는 영어를 이해할 수 있니?

11. You may not go to the bathroom
넌 화장실에 가면 안 돼.

12. I cannot[can't] feel my feet
난 내 발을 느낄 수 없어. (난 발에 감각이 없어.)

13. Can you watch TV
너는 TV를 볼 수 있니?

14. I cannot[can't] use the computer
나는 컴퓨터를 사용할 수 없어.

15. Can you be a pilot
너는 파일럿이 될 수 있니?

16. Can't Iron Man have superpowers without his suit
아이언맨은 그의 옷 없이 초능력을 가질 수 없니?

17. You may not have a seat
너는 자리에 앉으면 안 돼.

18. I cannot[can't] use my cell phone during class
나는 수업시간에 핸드폰을 쓸 수 없어.

19. I cannot[can't] keep a secret
나는 비밀을 지킬 수 없어.

20. Yujin may not come to school
유진이는 학교에 안 올지도 몰라.

Unit 03 조동사 must, have to (1)

Check and Write

▶ 본문 p.31

2. must 3. have to 4. had to 5. must

Unit 04 조동사 must, have to (2)

Check and Write

▶ 본문 p.33

2. must not 3. doesn't have to
4. don't have to 5. must not

Practice 1

▶ 본문 p.34

A 2. must not 3. have to[must] 4. must not
5. have to[must]

B 1. have to 2. have to[must] 3. must not
4. have to[must]

C 1. must[have to] 2. must[has to] 3. had to
4. have to 5. must[have to]

D 1. must[have to] 2. have to
3. must[have to] 4. must not

Practice 2

▶ 본문 p.36

2. Do I have to eat dinner
저 저녁 먹어야 해요?

3. I have to go home
나 집에 가야 해.

4. I have to have dinner

5. I have to call my mom
나 엄마한테 전화해야 해.

6. You must not skip meals
식사를 거르면 안 된다.

7. Do I have to wear pants
저 바지 입어야 해요?

8. You must follow the rules
넌 규칙을 따라야만 해.

9. Andy has to clean his room
Andy는 방을 청소해야 해.

10. You don't have to worry
너는 걱정할 필요 없어.

11. They must change the rules
그들은 규칙을 바꿔야만 해요!

12. He has to take care of

13. We don't have to be mean

14. It doesn't have to be a snowman
그게 눈사람이 아니어도 돼.

15. He has to change his clothes
그는 옷을 갈아입어야만 해.

16. You must try

17. We must forget

18. You must save power
너는 힘을 아껴야 해.

Practice 3

▶ 본문 p.38

2. I have to do my homework

3. You have to plant trees
당신은 나무를 심어야 합니다.

4. She has to drink milk
그녀는 우유를 마셔야 합니다.

5. You must not look at the sun

6. You must wear sunglasses
넌 선글라스를 껴야만 해.

7. I have to remember his name
난 그의 이름을 기억해야만 해.

8. Dad has to go
9. You must use a pencil
10. You have to raise your hand
11. He must not forget his passport
그는 그의 여권을 잊어서는 안 되겠네요.

12. You don't have to worry
13. He must bring
14. You must stop
15. My parents must buy
16. It doesn't have to be
17. My computer must have
18. You have to visit
19. You must not buy computers

Let's Practice More!

SET 01
▶ 본문 p.40

02. pay	03. turn	04. pay	05. swim
06. study	07. borrow	08. go	09. have
10. call	11. change	12. take	

SET 02
▶ 본문 p.41

02. must	03. O	04. don't	05. O
06. O	07. has	08. have	09. O
10. O	11. O	12. must	13. O
14. O			

SET 03
▶ 본문 p.42

02. must have	03. have to
04. has to	05. must be
06. have to pay	07. have to
08. have to get	09. have to
10. have to eat	11. has to
12. doesn't have to	13. must save
14. has to	

SET 04
▶ 본문 p.43

02. doesn't have to	03. must not
04. must not	05. don't have to
06. doesn't have to	07. must not
08. must not	09. don't have to
10. must not	11. must not
12. don't have to	

SET 05
▶ 본문 p.44

02. don't have to	03. O
04. O	05. O
06. O	07. must not swim
08. O	09. don't have to
10. don't have to	11. O
12. doesn't have to	13. O
14. doesn't have to	

SET 06
▶ 본문 p.45

02. must, get, up	03. have, to, remember
04. must, use	05. must, arrive
06. have, to, wear	07. must, follow
08. must, try	09. have, to, do
10. must, not, cross	11. have, to, pay
12. must, study	13. had, to, borrow
14. must, not, leave	

SET 07
▶ 본문 p.47

02. Andy has to pay for the beach umbrellas and chairs
Andy는 비치파라솔과 의자에 돈을 내야 해.

03. She has to put on sunblock
그녀는 자외선 차단제를 발라야 해.

04. Jane has to read the textbooks
Jane은 교과서를 읽어야 해.

05. We have to go to the library
우리는 도서관에 가야 해.

06. He has to wait for the dinner
그는 저녁식사를 기다려야 해.

07. Minji doesn't have to order dessert
민지는 디저트를 주문하지 않아도 돼.

08. She has to try the cheese pizza at this restaurant
그녀는 이 음식점에서 치즈 피자를 꼭 먹어 봐야 해.

09. He doesn't have to go
그는 갈 필요 없어.

10. Does Jisun have to eat dinner
지선이는 저녁을 먹어야 해요?

11. She has to go home
그녀는 집에 가야 해.

12. He has to have dinner with Jake
그는 Jake와 함께 저녁을 먹어야 해.

13. Does Jisun have to wear pants
지선이는 바지를 입어야 해요?

14. My sister has to follow the rules
나의 여동생은 규칙을 따라야만 해.

15. She has to try many times
그녀는 여러 번 시도해야 해.

16. You have to forget bad things
너는 나쁜 것들을 잊어야 해.

17. We have to drink milk
우리는 우유를 마셔야 합니다.

18. They have to bring me a gift
그들은 나에게 선물을 가져와야만 해요!

19. He has to buy me a new computer
그는 나에게 새 컴퓨터를 사줘야만 해.

20. She must stop here
그녀는 여기에서 멈춰야 합니다.

SET 08
▶ 본문 p.49

02. You had to save power
너는 힘을 아껴야 했어.

03. I will have to do my homework on a computer
나는 컴퓨터로 숙제를 해야 할 거야.

04. You will have to wear sunglasses
넌 선글라스를 껴야만 할 거야.

05. I had to remember his name

난 그의 이름을 기억해야만 했어.

06. You had to use a pencil on the answer sheet
여러분은 답안지에 연필을 사용하셨어야 합니다.

07. You will have to raise your hand to ask questions
여러분은 질문하려면 손을 들어야 할 것입니다.

08. You will have to visit the computer store
넌 컴퓨터 상점을 방문해야 할 거야.

09. You had to buy computers offline
넌 컴퓨터를 오프라인에서 사야 했어.

10. We had to arrive on time
우리는 제 시간에 도착해야 했어.

11. You will have to get up early
너는 일찍 일어나야 할 거야.

12. They had to worry
그들은 걱정해야 했어.

13. You will have to get a B
너는 B를 받아야 할 거야.

14. He had to bring me a gift
그는 저에게 선물을 가져와야만 했어요!

15. You had to stop here
여러분은 여기에서 멈춰야 했습니다.

16. I will have to water this plant
나는 이 식물에 물을 줘야 할 거야.

17. My computer will have to have a big screen
내 컴퓨터는 큰 화면을 가지고 있어야만 할 거야.

18. You will have to pay for parking
주차하려면 돈을 내야 할 겁니다.

19. You will have to be careful
조심해야 할 것입니다.

20. You had to read the textbooks
넌 교과서를 읽어야 했어.

Chapter 02 형용사

Unit 01 형용사의 종류와 역할 (1)

Check and Write ▶ 본문 p.55

3. sick 5. happy 6. green 7. strong
9. warm 10. soft 12. angry

Unit 02 형용사의 종류와 역할 (2)

Check and Write ▶ 본문 p.57

2. sick 3. white 4. hungry
5. sweet 6. shy

Practice 1 ▶ 본문 p.58

A 2. sour 3. famous 4. pretty
B 1. smart 2. cute 3. fast
4. slow 5. tiny
C 1. rainy 2. humid 3. windy
4. sunny 5. hot
D 1. kind 2. same 3. wonderful
4. important

Practice 2 ▶ 본문 p.60

2. I am angry
나 화났어!

3. You are famous
당신은 유명합니다.

4. You can't say anything nice
너는 어떤 멋진 것도 말할 수 없다.

5. I want a different result
나는 다른 결과를 원한다.

6. You are honest
너는 정직해.

7. Sunday is my favorite day
일요일은 내가 가장 좋아하는 날이야.

8. He is big and ugly
그는 덩치가 크고 못생겼어.

9. He looks strange
그는 이상해 보여.

10. I will be careful
제가 조심할게요.

11. Why are your hands dirty
왜 당신의 손은 지저분해요?

12. I am sleepy
나는 졸려.

13. I am not crazy
나는 미치지 않았어.

14. I am short
나는 키가 작아.

15. I don't have any special talents
나는 어떠한 특별한 재능도 가지고 있지 않다.

16. He is brave
그는 용감하다.

17. I am alone
나는 혼자야.

18. This is my new diary
이건 나의 새 일기장이야.

19. That is a bad choice
그건 나쁜 선택이구나.

20. We have good news

Practice 3 ▶ 본문 p.63

2. He is[He's] mean
그는 짓궂어.

3. Today is a hard day
오늘은 힘든 날이야.

4. The English test is difficult
영어 시험은 어려워.

5. I am[I'm] tired
나 지쳤어.

6. That is nice advice

그것 참 멋진 충고구나.

7. The dog has short legs
그 개는 짧은 다리들을 갖고 있어(다리가 짧아).

8. This milk is fresh
이 우유는 신선해.

9. The tortoise is slow
그 거북이는 느리다.

10. The cat is cute
그 고양이는 귀여워.

11. The park is beautiful
그 공원은 아름다워.

12. I am[I'm] hungry
나 배고파.

13. She is[She's] kind

14. Dogs are loyal
개들은 충직하다.

15. The car is expensive
그 차는 비싸다.

16. I want a yummy cake
나는 맛있는 케이크를 원해.

17. We are ready
우리는 준비가 됐어.

18. Jane has a good voice
Jane은 좋은 목소리를 갖고 있다.

19. The baby is lovely
그 아기는 사랑스러워.

20. He writes a long letter

Let's Practice More!

SET 01
▶ 본문 p.66

02. X	03. O	04. O	05. X
06. O	07. O	08. X	09. O
10. O	11. X	12. O	

SET 02
▶ 본문 p.67

02. slow	03. black coat	04. bad news
05. famous singer	06. friendly	07. full
08. dirty	09. easy	10. dark room
11. strange	12. good idea	13. windy day
14. short		

SET 03
▶ 본문 p.68

02. (s)our	03. (f)amous	04. (r)ainy	
05. (w)indy	06. (s)unny	07. (h)ot	08. (t)all
09. (b)eautiful	10. (s)hort	11. (w)arm	
12. (y)ellow	13. (t)hirsty	14. (c)ute	

SET 04
▶ 본문 p.69

02. 보어	03. 수식	04. 보어	05. 수식
06. 보어	07. 수식	08. 보어	09. 보어
10. 수식	11. 보어	12. 보어	

SET 05
▶ 본문 p.70

02. beautiful	03. difficult	04. lovely
05. strange	06. windy	07. smart
08. honest	09. careful	10. sleepy
11. kind	12. full	13. good
14. wonderful		

SET 06
▶ 본문 p.71

02. early dinner	03. special talents
04. good news	05. bad choice
06. new diary	07. something sweet
08. nice advice	09. short legs
10. nothing new	11. sweet candies
12. long letter	13. good voice
14. warm hugs	

SET 07
▶ 본문 p.72

02. The dog has short legs
그 개는 다리가 짧아.

03. You can say something nice
너는 상냥한 무언가를 말할 수 있어.

04. Do you like sweet candies
너는 달콤한 사탕을 좋아해?

05. I like warm hugs
난 따뜻한 포옹을 좋아해.

06. Jane has a good voice
Jane은 좋은 목소리를 갖고 있다.

07. He writes a long letter to his mother
그는 그의 어머니께 긴 편지를 쓴다.

08. That is nice advice
그것 참 멋진 충고구나.

09. Today is a hard day
오늘은 힘든 날이야.

10. We have good news for you
우리는 너를 위한 좋은 소식을 갖고 있어.

11. I want a different result
나는 다른 결과를 원한다.

12. I don't like windy days
나는 바람이 많이 부는 날을 좋아하지 않아.

13. Let's take a walk on a sunny day
맑은 날에 산책 하자.

14. That is a bad choice
그건 나쁜 선택이구나.

15. This is my new diary
이건 나의 새 일기장이야.

16. Sunday is my favorite day
일요일은 내가 가장 좋아하는 날이야.

17. We play soccer together on the same team
우리는 같은 팀에서 축구를 함께 해.

18. He is an important member of this team
그는 이 팀의 중요한 멤버야.

19. I don't have any special talents
나는 어떠한 특별한 재능도 가지고 있지 않다.

20. I like sour jelly like Trolli
나는 트롤리 같은 신 젤리를 좋아해.

SET 08
▶ 본문 p.74

02. Your hands are dirty
너의 손은 지저분해.

03. Your cat is cute
너의 고양이는 귀여워.

04. Janet is a pretty girl
Janet은 예쁜 소녀야.

05. That is nice advice
그것 참 멋진 충고구나.

06. It is[It's] too humid
너무 습하다.

07. The English test is difficult
그 영어시험은 어려워.

08. The dog has short legs
그 개는 다리가 짧아.

09. Sihu is kind
시후는 친절하다.

10. Your hamster is cute
너의 햄스터는 귀여워.

11. I am[I'm] full
난 배불러.

12. She is[She's] kind to her pets
그녀는 그녀의 애완동물들에게 친절해.

13. The baby is lovely
그 아기는 사랑스러워.

14. Today is a hard day
오늘은 힘든 날이야.

15. Jane has a good voice
Jane은 좋은 목소리를 갖고 있다.

16. This pizza smells good
이 피자는 맛있는 냄새가 나.

17. We have good news
우리는 좋은 소식을 갖고 있어.

18. He gets wonderful goals
그는 멋진 골들을 넣어!

19. He is[He's] an important member
그는 중요한 멤버야.

20. Dogs are loyal
개들은 충직하다.

Chapter 03 부사

Unit 01 부사의 기능과 모양

Check and Write
▶ 본문 p.79

2. busily 3. quickly 4. loudly 5. softly

Unit 02 주의해야 할 부사 / 빈도부사

Check and Write
▶ 본문 p.81

A 2. 형용사 3. 형용사 4. 부사
5. 형용사 6. 부사

B 2. am always 3. can never

Practice 1
▶ 본문 p.82

A 2. well 3. slowly 4. high
5. so 6. again

B 1. hard 2. together 3. quickly
4. loudly 5. happily

C 1. late 2. fast[quickly] 3. so
4. hard 5. quickly[fast] 6. later
7. always 8. exactly

Practice 2
▶ 본문 p.84

2. well 3. fast 4. hard 5. happily
6. loudly 7. too 8. easily 9. very
10. hard 11. still 12. slowly 13. very
14. even 15. Honestly 16. always
17. together 18. perfectly 19. usually
20. quickly

Practice 3
▶ 본문 p.87

2. fast
She walks fast
그녀는 빨리 걷는다.

3. already
It is already 11:00 p.m.
벌써 밤 11시야.

4. meet again
When can we meet again
우리 언제 또 만날 수 있지?

5. late
Junwoo wakes up late
준우는 늦게 일어난다.

6. is very
Our English teacher is very kind
우리 영어 선생님은 매우 친절하셔.

7. too dangerous
It's too dangerous
그것은 너무 위험하다.

8. go to school today
He can go to school today
그는 오늘 학교에 갈 수 있어.

9. early
He goes to school early
그는 학교에 일찍 가.

10. often says
Mom often says that
엄마는 그것을 자주 말해요.

11. really
I really like movies
난 정말 영화를 좋아해.

12. is still
He is still in the hospital
그는 아직도 병원에 있다.

13. safely
We cross safely at the crosswalk
우리는 안전하게 횡단보도를 건넌다.

14. never has
He never has breakfast
그는 아침을 전혀 먹지 않는다.

15. carefully

My aunt drives carefully
나의 이모는 조심히(신중하게) 운전하셔.

16. always takes
Mina always takes piano lessons
미나는 항상 피아노 수업을 들어.

17. seldom
She seldom eats chocolate
그녀는 초콜릿을 거의 먹지 않아.

18. strongly
He ties them strongly
그는 그것들을 단단하게 묶어요.

19. angrily
She speaks angrily
그녀는 화나서 말해.

20. speak loudly
You can speak loudly
너는 크게 말할 수 있어.

Let's Practice More!

SET 01 ▶ 본문 p.90

02. happily	03. safely	04. newly
05. sadly	06. quickly	07. simply
08. busily	09. angrily	10. loudly
11. terribly	12. softly	

SET 02 ▶ 본문 p.91

02. O	03. carefully	04. O
05. safely	06. O	07. heavily
08. O	09. O	10. gently
11. O	12. easily	13. O
14. angrily		

SET 03 ▶ 본문 p.92

02. well	03. high	04. together
05. hard	06. quickly	07. late
08. fast	09. exactly	10. loudly
11. really	12. again	13. happily
14. later		

SET 04 ▶ 본문 p.93

02. 부	03. 동	04. 형	05. 동
06. 형	07. 동	08. 부	09. 형
10. 동	11. 형	12. 동	

SET 05 ▶ 본문 p.94

02. 형	03. 부	04. 형	05. 형
06. 부	07. 형	08. 부	09. 형
10. 부	11. 부	12. 형	13. 부
14. 부			

SET 06 ▶ 본문 p.95

02. O	03. X	04. X	05. O
06. O	07. O	08. X	09. X
10. O	11. X	12. O	13. X
14. O			

SET 07 ▶ 본문 p.96

02. seldom eats	03. never has
04. am usually	05. often nags
06. usually go	07. often cries
08. are always	09. never studies
10. usually arrive	11. can never
12. usually play	13. often cleans
14. usually talks	15. always speak
16. always work	17. often go
18. is always	19. seldom lose
20. usually go	

SET 08 ▶ 본문 p.98

02. simply	03. easily	04. hard
05. heavily	06. late	07. again
08. later	09. fast	10. well
11. safely	12. well	13. carefully
14. early	15. Honestly	16. really
17. already	18. carefully	19. quickly
20. often		

Chapter 01~03 실전테스트 ▶ 본문 p.100

01. (1) must go (2) can go
02. You must do your homework.
너는 네 숙제를 해야만 해.
03. She can cook this soup.
그녀는 이 스프를 요리할 수 있다.
04. He has to speak English.
그는 영어로 말해야만 한다.
05. You may have a seat.
너는 앉아도 좋다.

06. (s)eldom	07. (a)lways	
08. (n)ever	09. (s)ometimes	
10. (o)ften	11. have, to	12. can
13. must	14. ②	15. ②
16. strange	17. beautiful	18. tall
19. ①	20. ③	21. ①
22. ①		

23. 형용사 - kind, rainy
부사 - always, honestly, happily

24. ③ easily	25. ③ nicely	26. ②
27. sometimes	28. never	
29. always	30. seldom	

Chapter 04 감탄문

Unit 01 What으로 시작하는 감탄문

Check and Write
▶ 본문 p.107

A 2. What 3. a 4. an
B 2. What an exciting game (this is)
(이건) 아주 흥미로운 놀이구나!

Unit 02 How로 시작하는 감탄문

Check and Write
▶ 본문 p.109

A 2. How, is 3. very 4. high
B 2. How happy he looks
그는 아주 행복해 보이는구나!

Practice 1
▶ 본문 p.110

A 2. what 3. How 4. spring
B 1. beautiful 2. How 3. What
4. well 5. ice cream 6. cold
C 1. How 2. very 3. What
4. kind 5. friend
D 1. question 2. How 3. What
4. very 5. nice

Practice 2
▶ 본문 p.112

2. How delicious it is
그것은 정말 맛있구나!
3. What a good idea
아주 좋은 생각이구나!
4. What a tall tree
매우 큰 나무구나!
5. How funny
정말 재미있구나!
6. How slowly she answers
그녀는 정말 천천히 대답하는구나!
7. How fast he runs
그는 참 빠르게 달리는구나!
8. What a wonderful day
아주 멋진 날이구나!
9. How great the dinner smells
저녁 식사 냄새가 참 좋구나!
10. What a waste of time
완전히 시간 낭비야!
11. What an honor
아주 영광스럽구나!
12. How well your mom cooks
너희 엄마는 요리를 참 잘하시는구나!
13. How clean
정말 깨끗하구나!
14. What a happy day
정말 행복한 하루구나!
15. What a pleasant surprise
정말 뜻밖의 기분 좋은 일이구나!
16. What a lovely voice
정말 사랑스러운 목소리구나!
17. How lazy the dog is
그 개는 정말 게으르구나!
18. What a lovely cat
정말 사랑스러운 고양이구나!
19. What a pity
참 애석한 일이구나!
20. How well she plays

Practice 3
▶ 본문 p.114

2. How well he plays the guitar
그는 기타를 참 잘 연주하는구나!
3. How beautifully she sings
그녀는 정말 아름답게 노래하는구나!
4. What a nice cover (it is)
(그것은) 아주 멋진 표지구나!
5. What an excellent picture (it is)
(그것은) 정말 훌륭한 그림이구나!
6. What a large library (it is)
(그것은) 정말 큰 도서관이구나!
7. How big (it is)
(그것은) 아주 크구나!
8. What a kind brother (he is)
(그는) 정말 친절한 오빠구나!
9. What a heavy rain (it is)
비가 정말 많이 오는구나!
10. How loudly they bark
그들은 매우 큰 소리로 짖는구나!
11. How gently he speaks
그는 정말 온화하게 말을 하는구나!
12. What a wonderful sister (she is)
(그녀는) 정말 멋진 누나구나!
13. How well you draw
너는 참 그림을 잘 그리는구나!
14. How tall (he is)
(그는) 정말 키가 크구나!
15. What a cute puppy (it is)
(그것은) 정말 귀여운 강아지구나!
16. How white its fur is
그것의 털이 정말 하얗구나!
17. How peaceful (he is)
(그는) 정말 평온하구나!
18. What a fast train (it is)
(그것은) 정말 빠른 기차구나!
19. How dark (it is)
정말 어둡구나!
20. How small his feet are
그의 발은 정말 작구나!

Let's Practice More!

SET 01
▶ 본문 p.117

02. 명 03. 형 04. 명 05. 형
06. 명 07. 부 08. 명 09. 부

10. 명 11. 형 12. 부

SET 02

▶ 본문 p.118

02. How 03. What 04. What 05. How
06. How 07. What 08. How 09. How
10. What 11. How 12. How 13. What
14. How

SET 03

▶ 본문 p.119

02. a 03. an 04. a 05. a
06. an 07. a 08. an 09. an
10. an 11. a 12. an 13. a
14. a

SET 04

▶ 본문 p.120

02. How great 03. How clean
04. What a happy day 05. How lazy
06. How well 07. What a good idea
08. How delicious 09. it is
10. you are 11. she is
12. his feet are

SET 05

▶ 본문 p.121

02. How loudly they bark
그들은 정말 큰 소리로 짖는구나!

03. What a kind girl she is
그녀는 정말 친절한 소녀구나!

04. What a large library it is
그것은 정말 큰 도서관이구나!

05. What a kind brother he is
그는 정말 친절한 남동생이구나!

06. What a heavy rain
비가 정말 많이 오는구나!

07. What a pleasant surprise it is
그거 정말 뜻밖의 기분 좋은 일이구나!

08. How well he plays the guitar
그는 기타를 참 잘 연주하는구나!

09. What a lovely voice it is
그것은 정말 사랑스러운 목소리구나!

10. How well your mom cooks
너의 엄마는 요리를 정말 잘하시는구나!

11. What an interesting book it is
그것은 정말 흥미로운 책이구나!

12. How beautifully she sings
그녀는 정말 아름답게 노래하는구나!

13. What a nice cover it is
그것은 정말 멋진 표지구나!

14. What an excellent picture it is
그것은 정말 훌륭한 그림이구나!

SET 06

▶ 본문 p.123

02. What a waste of time it is! 03. O
04. How broadly she smiles! 05. O
06. How kind she is!
07. What a good friend you are!
08. O
09. What a difficult question it is!
10. How nice she is! 11. O
12. What a fast train it is!
13. How small his feet are! 14. O

SET 07

▶ 본문 p.124

02. What delicious ice cream it is
그것은 정말 맛있는 아이스크림이구나!

03. What a beautiful day it is
정말 아름다운 날이구나!

04. How smart she is
그녀는 아주 똑똑하구나!

05. What hot weather it is
날씨가 정말 덥구나!

06. How well she swims
그녀는 정말 수영을 잘하는구나!

07. How cold it is
그거 정말 차갑구나!

08. How slowly she answers
그녀는 정말 느리게 대답하는구나!

09. What a wonderful day it is
정말 멋진 날이구나!

10. How fast he runs
그는 아주 빨리 달리는구나!

11. What a lovely cat it is
그것은 정말 사랑스러운 고양이구나!

12. How well your mom cooks
너의 어머니는 요리를 정말 잘하시는구나!

13. How beautiful she is
그녀는 매우 아름답구나!

14. How kind he is
그는 아주 친절하구나!

15. What a wonderful spring it is
아주 멋진 봄이구나!

16. How great the dinner smells
저녁 식사 냄새가 아주 훌륭하구나!

17. How big the elephant is
그 코끼리는 정말 크구나!

18. How lazy you are
너는 아주 게으르구나!

19. What a good idea it is
그것은 아주 좋은 생각이구나!

20. How white its fur is
그것의 털은 아주 하얗구나!

SET 08

▶ 본문 p.126

02. The room is very clean
그 방은 매우 깨끗해.

03. It is a very interesting book
그것은 아주 흥미로운 책이야.

04. She sings very beautifully
그녀는 매우 아름답게 노래해.

05. It is a very nice cover
그것은 아주 멋진 표지야.

06. It is a very happy day
매우 행복한 날이야.

07. The dinner smells very great
저녁 식사는 아주 훌륭한 냄새가 나.

08. It is a very tall tree
그것은 아주 큰 나무야.

09. It is very big
그것은 아주 커.

10. He is a very kind brother
그는 아주 친절한 형이야.

11. It is a very heavy rain
그것은 엄청난 폭우야.

12. It is a very pleasant surprise
그것은 정말 뜻밖의 기분 좋은 일이야.

13. They bark very loudly
그들은 매우 크게 짖어.

14. The dog is very lazy
그 개는 아주 게을러.

15. It is a very amazing day
아주 놀라운 날이야.

16. He speaks very gently
그는 매우 부드럽게 말해.

17. She is a very active girl
그녀는 아주 활발한 소녀야.

18. It is a very good idea
그것은 아주 좋은 생각이야.

19. You draw very well
너는 그림을 아주 잘 그려.

20. She plays hide-and-seek very well.
그녀는 숨바꼭질을 아주 잘해.

Chapter 05 명령문

Unit 01 긍정 명령문

Check and Write

▶ 본문 p.131

2. Be careful
조심해.

3. Look at me
나를 봐.

4. Take my hand
내 손을 잡아.

5. Cheer up
힘내.

Unit 02 부정 명령문

Check and Write

▶ 본문 p.133

2. Don't give up
포기하지 마.

3. Don't be late
늦지 마.

4. Don't fight with your brother
너의 남동생과 싸우지 마.

5. Don't cry
울지 마.

Practice 1

▶ 본문 p.134

A 2. Solve 3. Mark 4. Wait
5. Don't speak

B 1. Boil 2. Put 3. Cook
4. Be

C 1. Check 2. Don't worry 3. watch out
4. drive 5. get in

D 1. Come 2. Stop 3. Look
4. Put 5. Don't be
6. Don't bring

Practice 2

▶ 본문 p.136

2. Don't be afraid of mistakes
실수를 두려워하지 마세요.

3. Open your math textbooks
수학 교과서 펴세요.

4. Take out your pencils
연필을 꺼내세요.

5. Tell me the answer

6. Take a break
쉬세요.

7. Have some chocolate
초콜릿 좀 먹어.

8. Give me another one
하나 더 주라.

9. Be quiet and listen
조용히 하고 들어보세요.

10. Raise the volume
음량을 높여줘 .

11. Return to your seats
자리로 돌아가세요.

12. Don't raise the volume
음량을 높이지 마.

13. Bring your recorders

14. Come to my house

15. Don't bother me
나를 귀찮게 하지 마.

16. Be prepared

17. Don't pick the flowers
꽃을 꺾지 마세요.

18. Tell me the truth
나에게 진실을 말해줘.

19. Draw a circle on the paper
종이 위에 원을 하나 그리세요.

20. Don't forget your homework
숙제 잊지 마.

Practice 3

▶ 본문 p.139

2. Prepare the ingredients
재료를 준비해.

3. Give me the recipe

조리법을 나에게 (알려) 줘.

4. Write it down
그것을 받아 적어.

5. Don't talk so fast
너무 빠르게 말하지 마.

6. Put flour in a bowl
밀가루를 그릇에 넣어.

7. Add milk and eggs
우유와 계란을 추가해(넣어).

8. Bring some butter and sugar
약간의 버터와 설탕을 가져와.

9. Mix them well
그것들을 잘 섞어.

10. Don't mix too hard
너무 세게 섞지는 마.

11. Put it in the oven
그것을 오븐에 넣어.

12. Wait for 10 minutes
10분 기다려.

13. Be careful
조심해.

14. Go to the supermarket
슈퍼마켓에 가.

15. Don't buy any
아무것도 사지 마.

16. Ask me anything
뭐든 나한테 물어봐.

17. Don't worry too much
너무 걱정하지 마.

18. Don't leave the kitchen
부엌을 떠나지 마.

19. Don't forget the recipe
조리법 잊어버리지 마!

20. Clean the kitchen
부엌을 청소해.

Let's Practice More!

SET 01
▶ 본문 p.142

02. Solve	03. Don't	04. Be	05. Check
06. Don't	07. Get	08. Look	09. Be
10. Raise	11. Don't	12. Tell	

SET 02
▶ 본문 p.143

02. O	03. X	04. X	05. X
06. O	07. O	08. X	09. X
10. O	11. O	12. X	13. X
14. X			

SET 03
▶ 본문 p.144

02. Come to my house
우리 집으로 와.

03. Don't worry
걱정하지 마.

04. Cook for 5 minutes
5분 동안 익히세요.

05. Open your math textbooks
수학 교과서를 펴세요.

06. Be quiet and listen
조용히 하고 들어보세요.

07. Don't forget your homework
숙제 잊지 마.

08. Make some brownies for me
나를 위해 브라우니 좀 만들어줘.

09. Don't leave the kitchen
부엌을 떠나지 마.

10. Draw a circle on the paper
종이 위에 원을 하나 그리세요.

SET 04
▶ 본문 p.145

02. O	03. O	04. Drive
05. be	06. bring	07. O
08. Take	09. O	10. Give
11. O	12. mix	

SET 05
▶ 본문 p.146

02. Buy it
그것을 사.

03. Wait for 10 minutes
10분 동안 기다려.

04. Solve the problems
문제를 풀어.

05. Cook for 5 minutes
5분 동안 익혀.

06. Come here
이리 와!

07. Put it away
그것을 치워.

08. Take out your pencils
너의 연필들을 꺼내.

09. Explain this question
이 문제를 설명해줘.

10. Go to the supermarket tomorrow
내일 슈퍼마켓에 가.

SET 06
▶ 본문 p.147

02. 걱정하지 마세요	03. 떠나지 마
04. 조심하세요	05. 확인해봐
06. 가져오지 마	07. 두려워하지 마세요
08. 높여줘	09. 말하지 마
10. 와	11. 사지 마
12. 잊어버리지 마	13. 태워다주세요
14. 얘기하지 마세요	

SET 07
▶ 본문 p.148

02. Don't raise the volume
음량을 높이지 마.

03. Don't bother me
나를 귀찮게 하지 마.

04. Don't pick the flowers
꽃을 꺾지 마.

05. Don't forget your homework
너의 숙제를 잊지 마.

06. Don't get in the car
차에 타지 마.

07. Don't be afraid of mistakes

실수를 두려워하지 마.

08. Don't come here
이리로 오지 마!

09. Don't take out your pencils
너의 연필들을 꺼내지 마.

10. Don't take a break
휴식을 취하지 마.

11. Don't return to your seats
자리로 돌아가지 마.

12. Don't clean the kitchen
부엌을 청소하지 마.

13. Don't mark your answers with a black pen
너의 답을 검정색 펜으로 표시하지 마.

14. Don't speak during the exam
시험을 치는 동안 얘기하지 마.

15. Don't put noodles and sauce into the pot
면과 소스를 냄비에 넣지 마.

16. Don't open your math textbooks
수학 교과서를 펴지 마.

17. Don't tell me the answer for the second question
두 번째 문제에 대한 답을 나에게 말하지 마.

18. Don't bring your recorders for the next class
너의 리코더를 다음 수업시간에 가져 오지 마.

19. Don't come to my house after school
방과 후에 나의 집에 오지 마.

20. Don't talk so fast
너무 빨리 말하지 마.

SET 08 ▶ 본문 p.150

02. Wait until the time is up
시간이 다 될 때까지 기다려.

03. Don't draw a circle on the paper
그 종이에 원을 그리지 마.

04. Give me the recipe
나에게 조리법을 (알려) 줘.

05. Don't mix too hard
너무 세게 섞지 마.

06. Stop yelling
소리를 지르는 것을 멈춰.

07. Tell me the truth
나에게 진실을 말해 줘.

08. Don't buy it
그것을 사지 마.

09. Add milk and eggs
우유와 계란을 추가해(넣어).

10. Watch out for strangers
낯선 사람들을 조심해.

11. Don't look at this
이것을 보지 마!

12. Put it away
그것을 치워.

13. Don't be afraid
무서워하지 마.

14. Don't bring it home
그것을 집으로 가져오지 마.

15. Be prepared for anything
어떤 것에도 준비가 돼 있어야 해.

16. Don't leave the kitchen
부엌을 떠나지 마.

17. Come to my house
우리 집으로 와.

18. Don't forget the recipe
조리법을 잊지 마!

19. Bring some butter and sugar
버터와 설탕 조금을 가져와.

20. Take out a notebook
공책을 꺼내.

Chapter 06 청유문

Unit 01 청유문

Check and Write ▶ 본문 p.155

2. Let's 3. Let's not 4. Let's not 5. Let's

Unit 02 제안을 나타내는 다른 표현

Check and Write ▶ 본문 p.157

2. sing 3. not 4. making 5. don't

Practice 1 ▶ 본문 p.158

A 2. Let's 3. Why, not 4. Let's, not

B 1. Why, don't, you 2. How, about 3. put 4. Let's 5. Let's, not

C 1. Let's 2. How, about 3. Why, don't, we 4. Let's, not

D 1. Why, not 2. watch 3. Why, don't, we 4. How, about 5. buy 6. Let's, not

Practice 2 ▶ 본문 p.160

2. Let's go to the park
3. Why not wear this red skirt
이 빨간 치마를 입는 건 어때?
4. Let's not wear skirts
치마는 입지 말자.
5. Why don't you clean your room
네 방을 좀 치우는 건 어때?
6. Let's clean the room

7. How about playing soccer
8. Let's not waste time
시간을 낭비하지 말자.
9. Why not go home
10. Let's take a bus
버스 타자.
11. Why don't you walk home
걸어서 집에 가는 건 어때?
12. Let's go on foot
걸어서 가자.
13. Let's not leave anything
아무것도 두고 가지 말자.
14. How about coming back
15. Let's visit a museum
박물관에 가자.
16. Why don't you go back to your house
너희 집으로 돌아가는 건 어때?
17. Let's play a game
게임 하나 하자.
18. Why not take a picture
사진을 한 장 찍는 건 어떨까?
19. Why don't you stay with us
우리랑 같이 있는 건 어때?
20. Let's buy a present

Practice 3

▶ 본문 p.162

2. Why not watch a movie
영화를 보는 건 어때?
3. Why don't you check the weather
날씨를 확인해 보는 게 어때?
4. let's not go outside
5. How about going to the Han River
한강 가는 거 어때?
6. Let's do something different
무언가 다른 걸 하자.
7. Why don't you choose the menu
네가 메뉴를 정하는 건 어때?
8. How about ordering some pizza
9. let's not have it
10. How about playing video games
비디오 게임을 하는 건 어때?
11. Why not eat out
외식할까?
12. Let's go to the Thai restaurant
태국 음식점에 가자.
13. Why don't you get some rest
14. How about meeting at 5 o'clock
5시에 만나는 건 어때?
15. Let's not forget our plan
우리의 계획을 잊지 말자.
17. 너 내일 공원에 가는 건 어떠니?
18. 이제 이 실수를 잊어버리자.
19. 수현이네 집에서 놀자.
20. 가족과 함께 시간을 보내는 건 어때?

Let's Practice More!

SET 01

▶ 본문 p.165

02. O	03. O	04. do	05. O
06. not forget	07. O	08. make	
09. Let's not	10. O	11. O	12. clean

SET 02

▶ 본문 p.166

02. Let's play at Mina's house
미나네 집에서 놀자.
03. Let's go together
함께 가자.
04. Let's not leave anything
아무것도 두고 가지 말자.
05. Let's visit a museum
박물관에 가자.
06. Let's not be late
늦지 말자.
07. Let's forget this mistake
이 실수를 잊어버리자.
08. Let's not hurry
서두르지 말자.
09. Let's not fight about the menu
메뉴로 다투지 말자.
10. Let's go on foot
걸어서 가자.
11. Let's not watch an action movie
액션영화는 보지 말자.
12. Let's play a game
게임 하자.
13. Let's buy tickets
표를 사자.
14. Let's not go outside
밖에 나가지 말자.

SET 03

▶ 본문 p.168

02. Why	03. Why	04. How	05. Why
06. Why	07. Why	08. How	09. Why
10. Why	11. Why	12. How	13. How
14. Why			

SET 04

▶ 본문 p.169

02. How about ordering some pizza
피자를 좀 주문하는 게 어때?
03. Why don't you eat out
외식하는 건 어때?
04. Why don't you go to the mall with your sister
언니랑 같이 쇼핑몰에 가는 건 어때?
05. How about buying new clothes for her
그녀를 위해서 새 옷을 사는 건 어때?
06. Why don't you watch "The Jungle Book"
'정글북'을 보는 건 어때?
07. How about taking a break
잠깐 쉬는 건 어때?
08. How about cleaning your room
네 방을 좀 치우는 건 어때?
09. Why don't you play soccer at the park
공원에서 축구를 하는 건 어때?
10. How about walking home
걸어서 집에 가는 건 어때?
11. Why don't you come back tomorrow
내일도 또 오는 건 어때?

12. How about going back to your house
너희 집으로 돌아가는 건 어때?

SET 05

▶ 본문 p.170

02. Why not go to a movie together
같이 영화 보러 갈까?
03. Why don't you watch a horror movie
공포영화 보는 게 어때?
04. Why not wear this red skirt
이 빨간 치마를 입는 건 어때?
05. How about playing soccer at the park
공원에서 축구를 하는 건 어때?
06. Why not go home for dinner
저녁 먹으러 집으로 가는 게 어때?
07. Why don't you go back to your house
너희 집으로 돌아가는 건 어때?
08. Why not take a picture
사진을 한 장 찍는 건 어때?
09. Why don't you stay with us
우리랑 같이 있는 건 어때?
10. How about going to the Han River
한강 가는 거 어때?
11. Why don't you check the weather
날씨를 확인해 보는 게 어때?
12. Why not watch a movie
영화를 보는 건 어때?
13. How about playing video games
비디오 게임을 하는 건 어때?
14. How about ordering some pizza
피자를 좀 주문하는 건 어때?

SET 06

▶ 본문 p.172

02. O	03. eat	04. get	
05. meeting	06. O	07. go	08. go
09. take	10. stay	11. O	12. check
13. watch	14. playing		

SET 07

▶ 본문 p.173

02. 나가지마	03. 입어	04. 가자	
05. 다투지 말자	06. 타자	07. 낭비하지마	08. 보지 말자
09. 사	10. 늦지 말자	11. 먹지 말자	12. 입지마
13. 치우자	14. 가자	15. 타자	
16. 두고 가지마	17. 가	18. 가자	19. 해
20. 사자			

SET 08

▶ 본문 p.174

02. How about doing something different
무언가 다른 걸 하는 게 어때?
03. How about ordering some hamburgers
햄버거를 좀 주문하는 게 어때?
04. Why don't you choose the menu
네가 메뉴를 정하는 건 어때?
05. Why not eat out
외식할까?
06. Let's go to the Thai restaurant
태국 음식점에 가자.
07. Why don't you go to the park
공원에 가는 게 어때?
08. Let's not forget our plan
우리의 계획을 잊지 말자.
09. Why not go on a picnic
소풍 가는 건 어때?
10. Let's forget this mistake
이 실수를 잊어버리자.
11. Why don't you get some rest now
이제 쉬는 게 어때?
12. Let's play at Mina's house
미나네 집에서 놀자.
13. How about spending time with your family
너의 가족과 함께 시간을 보내는 건 어때?
14. Let's not worry about it
그것에 대해 걱정하지 말자.
15. Why not wear this red coat
이 빨간 코트를 입는 건 어때?
16. Let's not waste time
시간 낭비하지 말자.
17. Why don't you watch a horror movie
공포영화를 보는 게 어때?
18. How about traveling to France
프랑스로 여행을 가는 건 어때?
19. How about playing soccer at the park
공원에서 축구를 하는 건 어때?
20. Let's take a bus
버스 타자.

Chapter 04~06 실전테스트

▶ 본문 p.176

01. What	02. How	03. ④

04. My brother is (very) sick. 내 형이 (매우) 아프다.
05. What an old house this is! 이건 정말 낡은 집이야!

06. Don't[Do not]	07. ③	08. ①, ④
09. Let's	10. Don't[Do not]	
11. Please	12. Don't[Do not]	

13. ②, 산책을 하자
14. Be a nice person. 멋진 사람이 되어라.
15. Let's eat Japanese food. 일식을 먹자.

16. ③	17. ④

18. How well Mina sings! 미나는 정말 노래를 잘하는구나!
19. How → What
What old cars (these are)! (이것들은) 정말 오래된 차야!
20. ②
21. Don't lose your bag. 네 가방을 잃어버리지 마라.
22. Let's not see it. 그것을 보지 말자.
23. ③
24. ③, Don't begin your speech.
25. ③, Bring this to her.

26. ③	27. ④	28. ③
29. How, about	30. Why, not	

CH 06

Cultural Tips
재미로 익히는 문화상식

대부분의 나라는 표준시가 달라요!

Mina in Korea

Alex in America

대부분의 나라가 그 나라 고유의 표준시를 정해서 사용하고 있기 때문에 나라마다 시간이 달라요.
그렇게 나타나는 시간의 차이를 "시차"라고 한답니다. 그렇다면, 한국과의 시차가 없는 나라는 어느 나라인지 아나요?
바로 일본이에요. 한국과 일본은 표준시의 기준이 되는 선이 동경 135°선으로 일치하기 때문에 한국과 일본은 시차가 없답니다. 기억해두면 좋겠죠?

미국의 독특한 섬머타임제

Alex와 John은 미국에서 태어난 쌍둥이 형제예요.
John은 2016년 11월 6일 새벽 1시 58분에, Alex는 새벽 2시 1분에 태어났어요.

John이 먼저 태어났는데 왜 Alex가 형이냐구요?
그건 미국의 독특한 섬머타임제 때문에 벌어진 일이에요.
미국은 낮 시간을 활용해서 에너지를 절약하고 경제활동을 촉진시키기 위해 낮 시간이 길어지는 3월의 어느 일요일 새벽 2시가 되면 시계를 새벽 3시로 한 시간 빨리 맞춰 놓아요. 그렇게 약 7개월을 유지하다가 낮 시간이 짧아지기 시작하는 10월이나 11월의 어느 일요일 새벽 2시가 되면 반대로 시계를 새벽 1시로 한 시간 늦게 맞춰 시간을 원래대로 돌려 놓는 거예요.
섬머타임제가 시작되는 날과 끝나는 날은 해마다 조금씩 달라지는데 2016년에는 11월 6일 새벽 2시에 끝났어요!
섬머타임이 끝나기 전에 태어난 John은 그대로 새벽 1시 58분에 태어난 거지만, 섬머타임이 끝난 후 새벽 2시 1분에 태어난 Alex는 새벽 2시를 새벽 1시로 바꿔놓는 바람에 새벽 1시 1분에 태어난 셈이 되는 거예요.
그럼 Alex가 먼저 태어난 게 되죠?
독특한 섬머타임제 덕분에 이런 일이 벌어졌네요!

초등영문법 3800제 서평

초등3학년 아이.. 원서는 어느 정도 잘 읽는데.. 글씨 쓰는 걸 많이 어려워해요. 그래서 문법을 알면 도움이 되지 않을까 싶어서 찾다가 3800제를 만났네요. 초등 저학년 아이가 혼자서 하는데 있어서 어려움이 없어요. 쉬운 단어로 설명을 해주니 쉽게 이해하고 공책에 배운 걸 써보기도 하면서 혼자서 열심히 공부하고 있어요. 2번, 3번 쭈욱~~ 3800제로 나갈까 합니다. *YES24* / 은**주

형이 중학교 진학 전부터 중학생용 3800제를 풀고 있었고 3800제 구성이 만족스러워서 초등 동생도 풀기 시작했어요. 개념도 구체적이고 다양한 내용이 있어서 좋았어요. 지루하지 않게 그림이 자주 삽입되어 있으니까 덜 삭막해요^^ 무엇보다 다각도로 연습문제가 진짜진짜 많아요. 어설프게 알고 진도 나가면 나중에 다시 봤을 때 까먹게 되고 제대로 이해 못하게 되거든요. 다양한 방식의 문제를 풀면서 영어실력이 확장되는 게 느껴져요. 게임, 마크만 성실, 꼼꼼하게 하지 공부는 대충 해치우고 마는 아이인데 이 교재를 통해서 언젠가는 영어 실력이 차곡차곡 쌓이길 기대해봅니다. 뒷편에는 단어 공부, 받아쓰기 연습을 할 수 있는 것도 있어요. 아이 핸드폰에 mp3파일을 넣어주면 스스로 할 수 있겠더라구요. 아직은 진도를 빨리 빼느라 숙제주진 않았는데 방학 시작하면 이 한권으로 영어공부는 충분할 것 같습니다. 핸드폰이 게임, 유튜브 보는 것만이 아닌 공부할 적에도 사용하는 것이라는 것을 알게 되길~^^; *YES24* / 희*

잠수네로 별칭되는 엄마표 영어를 한 지 몇 년 되었는데 엄마가 너무 띄엄띄엄 지도하다 보니 아이 단어와 문법이 많이 약한 것 같아 문법 교재로 구매했습니다. Unit 시작할 때 단어가 스물 몇 개 있고 의미를 인지하고 있는지 셀프 테스팅 하도록 구성되어 있고 개념 문제 뒤 연습문제가 쭉 있어서 아이가 스스로 정리하며 공부할 수 있어요. 난이도는 쉬운 편이라 차라리 부담 없이 스르륵 풀 수 있어서 좋아요. *YES24* / d**rh0424

문법은 실제로 문장 속에서 활용해봐야 이해가 쉽기 때문에 예제 중심의 반복학습이 가능한 책을 찾다가 선택한 교재입니다. 여러 형식으로 문제 풀이가 다양하게 제시되어 있어 문제를 풀다보면 그 원리가 절로 체득되어 정말 좋습니다. 아직 문법이라는 추상적인 개념을 이해하기 어려워하는 초등학생들에게 좋은 교재에요. 기존에 기초 문법의 틀이 조금 잡혀 있는 학생들은 자습용으로도 좋고 처음 문법을 접하는 학생들에게는 단계적으로 심화되는 문제 구성을 차근차근 밟아가며 공부하기에 좋습니다. *YES24* / a**owa

아이 문법 학습을 위해서 구입을 하게 되었습니다. 큰아이 중학영문법 3800제를 가지고 학습을 한 경험이 있어 믿고 구입하게 되었는데 역시나 초등문법도 많은 연습문제로 아이들이 같은 내용을 꾸준히 반복 연습하게 구성이 되어있어서 마음에 듭니다. 초등학생용이라 글씨도 큼직큼직하고 페이지마다 빈공간도 많이 있어서 답답하지도 않아서 좋아요. 초등학생 아이들은 일단 글씨가 작고 빽빽하면 보면서 질려하는 경향이 있는데 이 교재는 그런 점에서는 후한 점수를 주고 싶네요. 단순 객관식 문제 풀이로 학습시키고 싶은 분들에게는 추천하지 않구요. 객관식 문제풀이가 단원 끝에 단원테스트에 조금 밖에 없어서요. 객관식 문제풀이가 아닌 아이가 문장을 만들면서 학습하기를 원하시는 분들에게는 강추합니다. 타 학습서들이 보통 초등문법을 2권 내지 3권에 끝내는 것을 이 초등영문법 3800제는 1권부터 8권까지에 연습할 부분을 나누어 놓았으니 얼마나 많은 반복을 시킬 수 있는지 권수만 봐도 알 수 있지요. 어쨌든, 초등학교 4학년 아이 8권까지 열심히 공부할 예정입니다. *YES24* / j**onim

정답은 뒷면에서 확인하세요.

Say and write.

그림에 알맞은 단어를 큰 소리로 말하고 빈칸에 써 보세요.

1.

s a m e

2.

sk ☐ ☐ ☐

3.

cr ☐ ☐ ☐

4.

n ☐ ☐ ☐

5.

pl ☐ ☐ ☐

6.

ch ☐ ☐ ☐

Say and write.

그림에 알맞은 단어를 큰 소리로 말하고 빈칸에 써 보세요.

1.

s a m e

2.

sk a t e

3.

cr a n e

4.

n a m e

5.

pl a n e

6.

ch a s e